Dealing with Testing Times

"Remaining Strong, Healthy and Happy in Crises"

Robert Elias Najemy

Strategic Book Group

Strategic Book Group
P.O. Box 333
Durham CT 06422
www.StrategicBookClub.com

ISBN: 978-1-60911-874-7

I offer this book to us all—
that we may live in love, health, and abundance

Contents

CHAPTER ONE

Remaining Healthy, Happy, and Positive during Testing Times

What do we mean by the phrase "testing times"? There are periods in all our lives when certain events and situations demand greater inner strength, courage, faith, stamina, energy, understanding, optimism, inner security, and self-confidence. These times may be of a personal, familial, social, or even global nature. It could be a personal illness or the illness of a loved one. We might have lost our job or other source of income, or we might have discovered that we need to work many more hours just to survive. We may have lost all of our savings in the stock market or have had to resort to declaring bankruptcy. We may have lost a limb or an important internal organ. A loved one may be going through a psychological crisis and have started behaving in irrational ways. We may have just found out that our spouse is cheating on us or that our child is taking drugs or is very unhappy. War, floods, fires, earthquakes, and other natural disasters are all testing times. And the most intense for us all is the loss of a loved one.

Today, we—as a global community—are going through a financial crisis in which many are being tested in myriad ways. Although everyone is, or will be, affected to a different degree, we are all passing through testing times concerning the economy, environment, and peaceful stability. The suggestions in this book are applicable to all types of testing times, regardless of whether they are personal or social.

It is very natural for us to feel concerned about our future when we see the economy taking a downturn, people getting laid off, basic needs not being met, and anger building up in many sectors of society. You, like many others, might naturally be feeling pain, fear, anxiety, betrayal, anger, and even hate toward those you believe are responsible for what has happened and is happening. These emotions, however, do not help us deal with the situation effectively. They disrupt and weaken our nervous, endocrine, and immune systems, thus compromising our health, vitality, clarity, and ability to deal effectively with life's pressures and demands.

1

Additionally, negative feelings attract to us—through the law of attraction and manifestation—even *more* of what we are feeling negative about. We energize and attract realities by fearing them or holding strong emotions toward them. In such cases, our relationships suffer while our pain and frustration continue to increase. Our thinking becomes more confused and we react compulsively, making less enlightened decisions.

During testing times we need to be very much in touch with our inner power and wisdom, so as to maintain our health, happiness, peace, love, and unity with our family and society. This is an opportune time to develop our inner wisdom, strength, and guidance. The essence of what we need to remember is that what is happening to us and around us is *not* a mistake or some kind of punishment. It is something that we have all chosen on a spiritual level as an opportunity to let go of old limiting beliefs, emotions, and values and move forward in our emotional, mental, social, and spiritual development. We have all chosen together (on a spiritual level) to create these times in order to give ourselves the opportunity to move forward individually and collectively. We have much to learn and much to gain by dealing positively with what is happening.

In this book, we offer a number of means for dealing with testing times more effectively and successfully, without fear or anxiety.

But before we continue, remember one simple fact: At this time, five billion people (80 percent) on this planet have been living all of their lives and will continue to live on less than $10 a day, which is $300 a month. Three billion of these people have been living, and will be living, on less than $2.50 a day ($75 a month), and 1.4 billion on only $37 a month.

The above statement in no way means that we should lower our standard of living, but we need to realize that these fellow souls are very likely *not any less happy* than you and I. They may even have less anxiety as they have very little to actually lose. They love and are loved by their families; they do things to gain their meager living; they eat simple foods; they rest; and they enjoy their free time in simple ways with family and friends. *They do not cry all day.* They probably laugh and smile as much as any of us.

Why is this important to know? The fact is that it is extremely unlikely that your life will ever be as economically challenged as theirs (especially if you employ some of the suggestions in this book); they are actually already living your worst nightmare and are not any less happy than you are. Keep this in mind as we explore ways in which you can maintain your health, happiness, and abundance during these testing times.

Remember that when we use the words "testing times," we are not only referring to the general economic, ethical, social, psychological, environmental, and spiritual crises that the global community seems to be going through but also to all personal or familial crises.

We have sought to keep this book as simple and easily employable as possible. You will learn effective ways to keep the body healthy and the mind clear as well as concepts that will enable you to be positive and confident even in difficult times. You will learn how to employ the laws of attraction and how to live in the present, free from the fear of the future and the bitterness of the past. You will also learn methods for letting go of anxiety and fear so as to experience clarity in all situations.

You will learn Ho'oponopono and other methods for positively interacting with the world. You will discover new and alternative ways of perceiving yourself, others, and life itself. This book is an invaluable handbook for dealing with life. Share it with friends and relatives.

CHAPTER TWO

Caring for Your Body

Your body and mind are the instruments with which you effectively create and enjoy all that you need to be happy. If your body becomes weak or ill, you will not be able to effectively and dynamically manifest the abundance and happiness that you desire. A weak or ill body will become an obstacle to your creative power.

Here are some simple steps to creating a healthy body:

1. Fresh Food – Eat as naturally as possible. Make sure you have plenty of fresh fruit and vegetables in your diet, and, if possible, choose organic food without pesticides, hormones, or other chemicals. Also, focus on whole grains as a source of energy and nutrition. Avoid lifeless or preserved foods and white sugar as much as possible.

2. Vitamin Supplements – During testing times you may need to take vitamins in order to strengthen your nervous system and mind. I suggest that you consider taking a multivitamin for one month so as to ensure that your nervous system has all the nutrients it needs, especially a vitamin B-complex for the nerves and vitamins A, C, and E for the immune system. Consult with your doctor if you have any food or substance sensitivities or any reason to believe that vitamins may not be good for you. Always read the instructions and admonitions on the labels before using.

3. Rejuvenate the Brain and Mind – Ensure a sufficient flow of blood, oxygen, and nutrients to the brain; it is the control center for your nervous system and your mental processes. This is especially important because many people simply do not get sufficient blood flow to their brain, which leads to less energy and clarity.

We can increase the flow of the blood to the brain by resting the head lower than the rest of the body. However, before performing any such exercise, you should consult with your physician to see whether increasing the blood circulation to the brain is appropriate for you.

Assume a head-low position once or twice a day for five to twenty minutes, thus gradually developing the ability to enjoy it without any discomfort. This allows fresh oxygenated blood and nutrients to rejuvenate all the cells of the brain, including the hypothalamus (controls the autonomic nervous system) and the pituitary gland (harmonizes the endocrine system and hormones). This rejuvenation leads to a stronger immune system and more dynamic health.

Also, head-low positions greatly improve our mental functioning. We feel more energized and can achieve greater mental clarity. Our emotional responses improve as well. We become more creative and effective in our decision making and actions. Our clarity and positive energy will certainly also benefit those around us.

One way to do this is with what we call the half shoulder stand.

If you have any doubts or physical problems, consult with your health professional before employing the following simple exercise.

Lie down on your back on your bed, or on a mat or blanket on the floor, with your buttocks close to a wall or any vertical surface and with your arms by your sides. If you find it more comfortable or want to bring more blood to the head and neck area, place a pillow or two underneath your buttocks.

Following the next steps according to your abilities and needs:

Stage 1 Inhale while raising your arms up over your head and, if possible, placing them on the horizontal surface behind you. Hold your breath in this position (not more than five seconds at first) and then start exhaling as you bring your arms up and back down by your sides. Do this ten times while counting mentally so that your inhalation, retention of breath, and exhalation are equal in duration.

Stage 2 Now inhale, hold your breath, and while exhaling turn your head as far as you comfortably can to the right. Hold it there a few seconds. Then inhale while returning your head to the center. Do the same to the left. Do this three times to each side alternately while again counting to ensure the inhalation, retention, and exhalation are equal in duration.

Stage 3 Continue to breathe slowly and deeply but comfortably without ever forcing your breath. Take five to ten comfortable breaths as you relax. You are bringing oxygen to your brain.

Stage 4 Simply relax in this position. With your eyes closed, relax the upper part of your body with special attention to your shoulders, neck, head, face, cheeks, eyes, and forehead. If you like, you can rest your hands on your abdomen or chest, or both.

Stage 5 Once the body is relaxed, you can then imagine healing energy flowing into the organs that need help. Imagine light, love, peace, and energy flowing into those organs and healing them. This is explained in detail in the next chapter.

Altogether, you will eventually be able to comfortably maintain this position for ten to twenty minutes.

Avoid this exercise if you have high blood pressure, a detached retina, or any other serious problem that contraindicates increased blood circulation into your brain or eyes.

In this position, blood flows down from the legs, alleviating various circulatory problems in the legs. The blood continues to flow through the liver, gall bladder, kidneys, and all other organs of the upper body. It then reaches the lungs, where it picks up more oxygen and flows into the neck, brain, pituitary gland, thyroid, and parathyroid glands. The muscles of the neck are now relaxed while all the organs are rejuvenated with a fresh supply of blood and oxygen.

As you are resting, at the end of this exercise, you can imagine healing energy flowing from your hands into your body healing and comforting the organs, even your emotions and mind. This is your time for self-nurturing, self-love and self-healing.

4. Self Massage – You can also spend some time in this position, or any other position, giving yourself a massage to your shoulders, neck, head, and face. This is actually very easy to do and will release physical and emotional blockages. Press on and gently rub the points on your shoulders, neck, head, and face that seem most sensitive and bring you the greatest sense of pleasure or release. This not only relaxes your muscles, but also frees up the blocked energy in your nervous system and energy system—as is known from the results of acupuncture. You can study these special energy points in the chapter on energy psychology.

Now we have four simple and easily employable ways of keeping your energy flowing freely, even when you are faced with challenging life situations. There is absolutely no reason to suffer physically because your external life situation is not as you would like it to be. You can remain positive and keep up your health and vitality. These simple guidelines are especially important when you are working many hours, sleeping less, or dealing with stressful situations.

There are many other ways to care for your body, including all forms of exercise: jogging, swimming, gymnastics, sports of all kinds, yoga, tai chi, breathing techniques, dance, and massage. Once you learn them, they are free if you do them on your own or perhaps a small fee if you join a community sports group.

Even in difficult times—and especially in difficult times—there is no reason you cannot enjoy exercising and getting your energy flowing. Worrying and becoming inert will not in any way improve your situation.

CHAPTER THREE

Strengthening the Mind

The mind—like any other organ, machine, or instrument—needs to be cared for, rested, tuned, and gradually improved. It is the organ, or instrument, with which you perceive life, express yourself, and actually *create* your life. When it is functioning well, you are able to think clearly, solve problems, be creative, and enjoy life.

The mind-improving techniques described below are forms of relaxation, positive visualization, and meditation. If you have a history of mental problems, please consult your health professional before performing or continuing these relaxation procedures.

1. Deep Relaxation – This can be done while sitting or lying down somewhere secure and comfortable. It is a process of relaxing all of your body and mind. Regardless of whether you are sitting or lying down, the spine should be straight with the neck and head in line with the spine while the arms and hands are placed comfortably and symmetrically to the sides of your body. The palms are best facing toward the sky unless you choose to place them on your abdomen or chest (or both). If you do so, make sure they are placed in a comfortable way so that no effort is required to keep them in that position.

You can then employ the following process:

   a. **Focus on your breathing** and mentally count so that the inhalation, retention, and exhalation of your breath have the same duration. Do not force the breath. Do this for about five minutes (not more at first). With each inhalation, imagine taking in peace and energy. With each exhalation, allow all tension and tiredness to dissipate.

   b. **Now allow your attention to move through your body** starting with the bottom of your feet and moving up toward the head, relaxing each part of the body as your attention passes through it. In this way, allow all the muscles of your body from the soles of your feet to the top of your head to relax. This should not be an effort, but rather an allowing or letting go.

c. And finally, as you **mentally count back from ten to one**, allow your body and mind to relax ever more deeply with each number.

CDs and mp3 files with a variety of guided relaxations can be found at *www.HolsticHarmony.com.*

Once you have allowed your body and mind to relax, you can then perform a number of mental exercises. Some of these are as follows:

1. **Visualize a healing and rejuvenating light** moving through your body, creating health, peace, and vitality in each and every part of your body. Then focus this healing light in specific parts of your body that need special help. If you do not see the light, simply imagine or feel that it is there.

2. **Focus on positive thoughts and images** concerning yourself, your life, and your contact with the world around you. Imagine yourself as you would like to be physically, emotionally, mentally, and spiritually. Your thoughts actually create your reality.

3. Be sure to always create feelings of **self-acceptance, self-love, and self-confidence.** These are essential assets in dealing with people and life.

4. Focus on your **perception of the Divine**—with or without form. Feel that **personal connection of love and gratitude** with the Divine.

5. **Ask a question** to be answered by your inner self. State the question three times and then be silent. The answer might come during deep relaxation or some time later, perhaps in a dream, upon waking, while reading, or conversing with someone.

6. This state can be used as a means to **access the contents of your subconscious** and perhaps the source of certain fears. This, however, should only be done with the guidance of a trained professional.

7. Leave time for your mind to **just be empty**. Let whatever changes need to take place in your body and/or mind to happen without your mental intervention. This time of emptiness is essential both in self-healing and in your spiritual growth process.

The following guidelines are also to be observed when employing a relaxation technique:

1. You should be **appropriately covered** in case your body's metabolism falls and you feel cold.

2. It is best to **be alone** in the room unless the other person is sleeping or is aware of what you are doing and capable of being extremely quiet. But if these conditions are not available, then go ahead and try to do deep relaxation anyway. You will be amazed by how much you can go within yourself and become unaware of what is going on around you.

3. **Leave time** to wake up and gradually move into activity. Do not come out of the relaxation just moments before you have to do something or be somewhere. Leave at least five minutes transition time, which is enough for most people.

4. If you suffer from **low blood pressure** and find that you get dizzy or feel cold after deep relaxation, then try doing your relaxation with your legs on top of a pillow or on the wall. In these positions, you will ensure an abundant blood flow to the brain and you will not feel dizzy or weak afterward.

5. **Do not overdo** relaxation. Twenty to thirty minutes twice a day is enough. Do not do more than this without the guidance of someone experienced in these techniques. Yoga teachers can help you, and a growing number of psychologists are using such techniques with their patients.

6. Relaxation techniques are best done on an **empty stomach**. However, they can be done after a meal if there is absolutely no other time. Some people who have trouble sleeping use them at night in order to fall sleep. Others who wake up early use these techniques to start their day off with a fresh and positive outlook. Experiment and find out what is best for you.

7. The purpose is not to fall asleep, but if you are tired and fall asleep, do not worry. If you fell asleep with a CD, the messages on the CD have been recorded by your subconscious mind. If you were working on your own, then at least you have relaxed and rejuvenated your body and mind.

8. Relax deeply at least once a day. Do not let your mind fool you into believing that there is no time: there is. You can eliminate something else that is offering you less in your life and replace it with relaxation.

9. Do not be put off or afraid if in the beginning you have **various negative side effects** after a relaxation session. This is simply the excess suppressed tension that you have bottled up within you and that is coming out in the form of negative symptoms. The symptoms may be yawning, headaches, dizziness, a feeling of irritability, or the need to cry or laugh nervously. You may feel pains in various parts of your body that were not there before; they were in the emotional and energy level that you do not normally feel. Or, you may feel nothing at all. In 80 percent of the cases, people feel wonderful.

If you are amongst the 20 percent who have a negative reaction at first, **do not fear**; this usually happens only a few times in the beginning, and then it passes. If you do not feel well, or have a history of mental problems, consult your health professional before performing or continuing these relaxation procedures.

There are CDs and mp3 files available at www.HolsticHarmony.com for self-therapy, self-acceptance, self-confidence, becoming more loving and peaceful, sending light to various parts of your body, and basic relaxing. You may also like to create your own CD with specific messages that you may feel are more suitable for your needs.

CHAPTER FOUR

Cultivating Positive
Thoughts and Feelings

You need a peaceful, clear, and positive mind in order to manifest your needs for yourself, your family, and perhaps even for society and the world.

Our emotions have a direct effect on our bodies. Every time we feel an emotion, our endocrine system excretes certain hormones or peptides, which flow through our bloodstream to all of our cells exciting them with the hormones associated with this emotion. The hormonal state created by negative emotions creates an imbalance in our nervous, endocrine, and immune system, which in turn creates an imbalance in all other systems as well. Subsequently, we are much more susceptible to illness and discomfort. Medical studies at the Institute of HeartMath Institute in California have shown that five minutes of anger or frustration can weaken aspects of the immune system for up to five hours, whereas five minutes of love or gratitude can strengthen the immune system for five hours.

Other studies have shown that we become chemically addicted to the hormonal excretions produced by certain emotions. We tend to subconsciously seek ways to recreate those feelings and their respective hormonal doses. We actually become chemically addicted—just like to any other addictive substance—to feeling fear, anger, hurt, bitterness, hate, or guilt, attracting and creating situations in which we can once again experience those familiar emotions. This leads to a vicious circle of recreating negative emotional states that reinforce our false beliefs that we are in danger, that we are victims or are unworthy. As a consequence, our health, relationships, work, and happiness deteriorate.

Our mind creates our reality.

Perhaps the worse result is that, because of the law of attraction, our negative feelings and thinking attract more of what we are feeling negative about. This might also be called the law of mirroring, sympathetic

12

vibration, or the law of manifestation. Regardless of what you call it, our mind, thoughts, emotions, expectations, and behaviors actually create our reality. When we change them, our reality then changes. In the same way that negative thoughts and feelings attract and create negative realities, so do positive thoughts and feelings attract and create positive realities.

This is the test of our times: to feel confident and positive even when our external reality does not inspire positive thinking. This is where the centered will be separated from the fearful. Those who are able to continue to feel confident in their ability to deal with and overcome challenges will do well. Those who succumb to fear, anxiety, anger, and hate—as it is very easy to do—will suffer even more.

Others mirror our emotions.

We broadcast our emotions whether we express them or not. These energies trigger others to react and behave in ways that reflect our emotions. When we submit for lengthy periods of time to intense negative emotions (not just momentary feelings, which are natural and harmless), we actually increase the possibility that others will behave negatively toward us.

Even when we are "innocent" and have done no harm to anyone, our fear of others will subconsciously invite them to behave in ways that mirror our fears. The same is true for our feelings of anger, guilt, pain, betrayal, hate, bitterness, rejection, criticism, and all other negative feelings. So I repeat once again: such emotions actually increase the possibility of attracting what we feel negatively toward.

This is an extremely important fact to remember when going through testing times. We are in fact being tested on our ability to remain positive by feeling worthy, secure, and powerful within ourselves, thus enabling ourselves to be courageous and positive in dealing with people and situations.

The power of gratitude.

One way to generate positive feelings is to focus on all we have that we can feel grateful for. Even when we do not have everything that we want or believe that we must have in order to feel happy, we can always focus on what we *do* have. When we concentrate only on what we do not have, we lose sight of all that we actually do have. As a consequence we do not allow what we already have to give us pleasure, security, and happiness.

We may not have the money or material security that we would like to have, but we may have people that we love and who love us. We may have good, or at least sufficient, health to enjoy life. We may have shelter and food. We may have electricity and running water. We may even have hot running water. If we have books and a TV, then we are probably in the top 20 percent of the well-off people of the world. If we have even a little money in the bank, then we are in the top 8 percent of the population.

We can feel grateful for the air we breathe, the flowers, trees, and birds around us. And, if we live near a park, forest, mountain, or any body of water, then we can find pleasure in their presence in our lives. Even in difficult times, we can enjoy the people, animals, and nature around us.

If we know how to read and have gained various forms of knowledge, then we are very special and blessed. If we have access to the Internet, then we are amongst the fortunate 6 percent of the planet who have access to a computer. If we have a telephone, we are better off than the three billion people (50 percent of the planet) who do not have one and may not even have seen one.

Feeling gratitude for all that we do have attracts more of what we need. When we feel gratitude, we broadcast positive energy that then mirrors back to us from other people and the universe in the form of more of whatever causes us to feel gratitude. When we feel lucky to have what we have, we attract more of whatever makes us feel lucky. On the other hand, when we feel unloved, unlucky, and discouraged, we attract more of whatever causes us to feel those negative feelings.

Life is a mirror that reflects back to us our past and present dominant thoughts, feelings, and behaviors. The power to create a new and happier reality, even in these testing times, stems from our ability to remain confident that we are always worthy and safe, and that we have the power and inner stamina to deal with and benefit from each and every challenge that life brings us.

It is important to perceive life as friendly rather than as dangerous. We have learned and become programmed to see life as difficult and unsafe. This is because for many thousands of years society has identified with the body and mind, ignoring our spiritual selves and the actual reason we, as spirit, are in these temporary bodies.

Nothing is by chance.

One basic change we need to make in the way we think is to realize that nothing in our lives ever happened by chance, nothing is now happening by chance, and nothing will ever occur by chance. We are loved beyond measure by the Divine, life, and the universe. Everything that happens in our lives occurs as an opportunity for our growth and evolution. We create these events and situations either with our unenlightened choices, feelings, and thoughts or as soul choices before we are born.

The reality is that we are actually immortal, formless consciousness temporarily occupying a body for the purpose of remembering our true eternal nature and manifesting in this material level harmony, love, unity, and beauty that already exist in our spiritual self. Having this in mind, there are only two reasons why something unpleasant happens in our lives: one is that we, in our ignorance and fear, are attracting negative realities, and the other is that on a spiritual level we have chosen this experience as an opportunity to wake up.

We can assume that these economic, social, and ethical crises the world is experiencing is a product of both causes. On one level, it is the result of our ego identification, selfishness, greed, fear, and alienation. On the other hand, it is what we have chosen now as an opportunity to develop inner security and greater feelings of unity, love, and cooperation.

We are personally loved.

We have all together, as humanity, created and chosen this situation as an opportunity to take our next step toward spiritual freedom from fear by creating a deeper connection with our unlimited inner power. Based on this perception, we can now begin to understand and feel that we are each personally loved unconditionally by the Divine and the universe.

There is nothing that has ever happened to us, or is now happening, or will ever happen in the unfolding of our lives that is not our creation—whether by our ego choices or by our soul choices. There is no such thing as punishment. There is no danger. Nothing can happen by chance. Nothing will ever happen that is not in our ultimate benefit as souls seeking to remember our true selves in these material bodies, where we have lost that feeling of formless immortality.

Every event, every outcome is an expression of love from the universe giving us the opportunity to realize the truth or to ignore it. We have free will. We can use these experiences for our ultimate purpose: to discover greater inner worth, security, freedom, and fulfillment. Or we can sink into fear, discouragement, pain, bitterness, resentment, anger, guilt, hate, and helplessness. This is our free will. These events have been created by our previous and present thoughts, words, actions, and soul choices in conjunction with the lessons we have chosen personally and communally to learn at this point in our evolutionary process. How we use and react to these events and situations, though, is our free choice. This is the choice we have in times of testing.

There is no divine punishment.

We must not confuse, as we have for thousands of years, the opportunities offered by these tests that we have set up for ourselves with any type of punishment. There is *no* divine punishment. This is an illusion. How could a divine being of unconditional love, who asks us to love even our enemies, ever have negative feelings toward or punish his or her creations, which are actually projections of itself on the material plane? It doesn't make any sense. The idea of punishment from God or the universe is an old, rather childish, perception of the Divine that has lost its usefulness as we move forward to realizing and manifesting our own inner divine potential.

Those who, until now, have believed that we are weak and unworthy sinners may benefit from learning that the actual goal of Christianity, as expressed by the early church fathers, is "theosis," or the process of becoming "Godlike." By freeing ourselves from fear and guilt, we bring forth our inner spiritual values such as love, peace, just action, truthfulness, nonviolence, selflessness, and compassion and service for others. These qualities manifest the "image of God," which is the potential within us all, as the "likeness of God" in our lives; this is the basic step in "theosis"—becoming like God while in a body.

It is essential that we free ourselves from the feeling that we live in a difficult, unfriendly, and punishing universe. We need to let go of these less evolved perceptions now to realize that we, altogether (all souls incarnated and not), comprise the being we call God. We are expressions of Divine Consciousness in these temporary physical bodies. We are the creators of our personal reality and co-creators of our social, national, and planetary realities.

Learning and manifesting.

We are in a process of learning to manifest ever more positive realities with abundance, peace, equality, love, and happiness for all; this is our life purpose. We have accepted to forget our true formless self in order to temporarily identify with the body and mind. In the highest levels of our being, we love everyone—even those who harm and disturb us. Our ego might not love them, but *we do* love them. Christ asks us to love even those who harm us because, by doing so, we are connecting to our true spiritual self, who actually already loves the others and cannot do otherwise.

When we realize that we live in a loving reality, we will feel secure and peaceful in all situations, and we will be able to help those around us do the same. Our energy will then be diverted from fear, resentment, and anger toward seeking solutions personally and collectively. We will be much more effective in creating the security, abundance, and happiness we seek.

You can do this by realizing and remembering the following:

1. You are, actually, an immortal Divine Consciousness who has temporarily projected your consciousness into your body. There is no birth, only a temporary projection of your consciousness into this body and mind. You were actually never born and will never die.

2. One day, you will simply retract your consciousness from your body at a time that you choose, which may happen slowly or suddenly. Regardless of the conditions of your withdrawal, you cannot and will not retract your consciousness from your body until your *own* chosen time. Even in the extreme possibility that someone might "murder" you, it can only happen with your *own* inner concurrence—which of course your ego and mind will have no awareness of.

3. The same is true for all the events that have occurred and will occur in your life. Nothing happens that you have not in some way created or chosen on some level. Everything that has happened, is happening, and will ever happen is always the best opportunity for your growth and awakening to the truth. You can be at peace with the fact that only that which serves your best possible interest as a soul in the process of your evolution will ever take place.

(4.) All of your loved ones are also eternal, immortal fellow souls who have chosen to play their temporary roles in your life drama (as you are playing your role in theirs) and who have chosen their own experiences and lessons. Nothing is happening or will happen in their lives that is not what they are freely creating and choosing as opportunities for learning their own chosen lessons. They, too, have free will to learn or to not learn. They may have to create more pain before they are ready to learn. Sometimes we can help them, and other times they are not open or ready for help. This is something we need to accept and be at peace with.

Worrying or fearing for our loved ones only undermines their own sense of power and self-confidence. We can help them much more effectively by perceiving them as eternal, powerful, and spiritual beings who have chosen their own life lessons and challenges and by believing in their ability to deal with and benefit from those tests.

There is a story (which I believe is true) about a man who saw a butterfly struggling to get out of its cocoon. The man decided to help the butterfly by cutting the cocoon open with his penknife, allowing the butterfly to get free with no effort at all. However, the butterfly could not fly because only through the effort of pushing with its wings on the walls of the cocoon could the wings become strong and develop for flying. And so, the butterfly remained earthbound.

Due to our love and concern for our loved ones, and especially our children, we often make the mistake of solving their problems for them so that in the end they have no wings to fly with. The best way to help our loved ones is to perform Ho'oponopono (which we will discuss later) and to visualize them filled with the inner light of their own true spiritual self in order to energize them with power and inner guidance.

Every time you find yourself fearing for, or worrying about, loved ones—if you really want to help them—gently direct your mind to the image of them with light, power, and inner guidance. This way you will empower them rather than participate in the illusion of their weakness. This is the greatest help we can offer a loved one.

5. Your opportunities for growth and evolution come in doses that may stretch your spiritual muscles but will not damage them unless you choose to ignore your inner power. For comparison,

if we want to increase the weight we can lift, there is no sense in lifting the same weights we have been lifting for years. We need to increase the weight enough to challenge us but not so much that we will break our backs trying. In the same way, we choose opportunities for growth that test our spiritual muscles in doses that we have the power to deal with. You will never be given a growth opportunity that is beyond your ability to handle. You have the free will, however, to access your inner power or to ignore it and feel weak, thus allowing the event or situation to drag you into pain, fear, despair, depression, and helplessness. Some people, after suffering or succumbing to fear at first, will then recoup and reconnect to their inner power, while others do not. *It is your choice.*

6. All events and realities are personally created—even in all-encompassing catastrophes. Christ mentioned when talking about the second coming that "Two men will be in the field, one will be taken and one will remain. Two women will be at the mill, one will be taken and one will remain." This means to me that even in a massive catastrophe—whether it be an earthquake, flood, fire, or an economic crisis—what happens to each individual will be what that specific soul needs at that particular time. Nothing will happen to you merely because it is happening to others. Regardless of what is occurring to others around you, only what you have chosen and created will happen to you. An event like a plane crash kills many people because that is the way that each one of them has chosen to withdraw their consciousness from their temporary physical body. If some have a ticket for the flight but have not chosen that means of withdrawal, they will, in some way, be obstructed from getting on that flight while others, not listed on the flight but who have chosen that means of departure will suddenly get on that flight.

Once we begin to think in this way, we will start to experience inner peace and clarity. We will realize that we live in a loving universe and we are loved unconditionally by the Divine, of which we are a part of. We will feel gratitude and perceive every challenge as an opportunity for a deeper reconnection with our true self. We will then manifest all of the abundance, health, joy, and love that we wish to have.

CHAPTER FIVE

Using Energy Psychology to Get Free from Fear, Anxiety, and Other Negative Emotions

In the last thirty-five years a number of new forms of psychotherapy have become very popular among psychologists, psychiatrists, medical doctors, and other health professionals who work with human emotional, mental, physical, and spiritual harmony.

Just a few of these methods are listed here:

TFT – Thought Field Therapy

EFT – Emotional Freedom Techniques

BSFF – Be Set Free Fast

TAT – Tapas Acupressure Technique

EMDR – Eye Movement Desensitization and Reprocessing

WHEE – Wholistic Hybrid of EFT and EMDR

Sedona Method

Freeze Frame – from the Institute of HeartMath

Ho'oponopono – from the spiritual teachers of Hawaii

We will label these methods generically as "energy psychology." In this book we will discuss in more detail EFT (Emotional Freedom Techniques), developed by Gary Craig.

What Health-Care Practitioners around the World Say about EFT

"EFT offers great healing benefits." Deepak Chopra, MD.

"I frequently use EFT for my patients with great results . . . Some day the medical profession will wake up and realize that unresolved emotional issues are the main cause of 85 percent of all illnesses. When they do, EFT will be one of their primary healing tools . . . as it is for me."

Eric Robins, MD, co-author of *Your Hands Can Heal You*.

"EFT has been, for me, the single most effective technique I've used in my forty-five years of practice as a psychiatrist. I've had success with panic, social anxiety, and many other disorders."

Curtis Steele, MD, Canada.

"In my fifty years as a practicing psychiatrist, EFT has proven to be one of the most rapid and effective techniques I've ever used."

Henry Altenberg, MD, USA.

"EFT is at the forefront of the new healing movement."

Candace Pert, PhD, author of *Molecules of Emotion*.

"By removing emotional trauma, EFT helps heal physical symptoms too."

Norm Shealy, MD, author of *Soul Medicine*.

"EFT is destined to be a top healing tool for the 21st Century."

Cheryl Richardson, author of *The Unmistakable Touch of Grace*.

"EFT is a simple, powerful process that can profoundly influence gene activity, health, and behavior." Bruce Lipton, PhD, author of *The Biology of Belief*.

"EFT is easy, effective, and produces amazing results. I think it should be taught in elementary school." Donna Eden, co-author of *The Promise of Energy Psychology*.

"The EFT is working just great for me, it is night thirteen of falling asleep without the pain of the Invisible Chronic Illness (fibromyalgia) and this is a phenomenal record for me. Since 1991, the onset of this illness, I have not had two pain free nights in a row. You are very much appreciated and a great big 'Thank you.'" Janet Cole

"In addition to several emotional issues, I have used EFT for impressive relief for many physical problems including hiatal hernia, candidiasis, and rheumatoid arthritis. The process is gentle and often provides benefits where other methods fail." Raul Vergini, MD, Italy

"I have found EFT to be so useful that it has become the centerpiece of my practice. I have used it successfully on a long list of emotional issues, including paranoid schizophrenia. Interestingly, when the emotional issues subside, physical ailments often enjoy simultaneous relief. I have seen this with the symptoms of fibromyalgia and MS as well as for swallowing problems, back pains, hemorrhoids, acidity, breathing problems, stomach pain, vaginitis, headaches, joint pains, and stomach problems." Sonia Novinsky, PhD, Brazil

Here is a partial list of psychosomatic problems that have responded positively to EFT:

◆ Weight Loss ◆ Anxiety/Panic Attacks ◆ Eating Disorders ◆ Relationship Issues ◆ Anger Management ◆ Children's Behavior ◆ Dyslexia ◆ Allergies ◆ Carpal Tunnel Syndrome ◆ Asthma ◆ Insomnia ◆ Multiple Chemical Sensitivities ◆ Pain Management ◆ Women's Issues ◆ Men's Issues ◆ Low Self-Worth/Self-Esteem ◆ Abundance ◆ Sports Performance ◆ Spiritual Connection ◆ Phobias ◆ War Trauma (PTSD) ◆ Sexual Abuse Trauma ◆ Addictions ◆ Depression ◆ High Blood Pressure ◆ Fibromyalgia ◆ Migraine Headaches ◆ Chronic Fatigue ◆ Obsessive/Compulsive Disorder ◆ Cancer ◆ Parkinson's Disease ◆ Muscular Dystrophy ◆ Multiple Sclerosis ◆ Rheumatoid Arthritis ◆ Cystic Fibrosis ◆ Diabetes ◆ Hepatitis C ◆ ALS—Lou Gehrig's Disease

Common Aspects of Energy Psychology

Regardless of their different approaches, all forms of energy psychology have some of the following aspects in common:

1. We can employ them by ourselves on ourselves.

2. These methods, as a rule, generate quick and often permanent results.

3. They can be employed directly on any emotions, including fear, anxiety, anger, guilt, bitterness, and rejection.

4. They can be used on physical pain and to reduce physical symptoms and, in some cases, remove even the causes of psychosomatic illness.

5. They can also aid us in getting free from chemical addictions such as to nicotine, caffeine, sugar, chocolate, and even heavy drugs.

How is this done?

1. We focus on the emotional or physical disturbance we want to release and evaluate how intense it is. We establish the **Subjective Units of Disturbance**, in which we evaluate the intensity of our emotion, desire, or physical discomfort from 0 to 10, where 0 means there is no disturbance at all and 10 means that the disturbance is extremely high. In this way, we develop the ability to objectify the disturbance as something separate from ourselves, and have a sense of how much it increases or decreases, or whether the problem exists at all.

2. The second step is to **accept whatever we are feeling** and to accept **ourselves** with whatever we are feeling. Acceptance is essential for freeing up the energy for change. We can use an affirmation like "Even though I have this _____ (specific emotion or problem), I love and accept myself." This is done in order to let go of any shame or anger that we have concerning our feelings. Some of us tend to suppress or ignore our emotions.

3. The next step is to be **willing to let go** of the emotion or disturbance. This is not always easy. We may have a subconscious need to hold on to our pain, anger, or problem for various reasons that are discussed in detail in the book *Free to Be Happy with Energy Psychology* and at www.HolisticHarmony.com.

4. We then **focus directly on the emotional or physical disturbance** concerning a certain stimulus, such as an event, behavior, situation, idea, or even a thought about the past or future. The disturbance might also be the result of chemical or hormonal changes.

Each particular emotion or state of mind is a **habituated energy structure,** which was learned in the past and reproduces itself whenever our older programmed brain synapses are activated, creating the message that we are in danger. In spite of our logic and wisdom, we are forced by these habituated energy fields—created by our outdated, but certainly active, programming—to feel anxiety, fear, hurt, anger, and guilt along with the repercussions of these emotional disturbances on our bodies, minds, relationships, and happiness. This is especially true when we believe, either subconsciously or consciously, that our security, self-worth, freedom, or pleasures are in danger.

5. The next step is to **change our energy state** while we are focused on the particular emotion, disturbance, physical pain, or discomfort. This is done in various ways, depending on the particular technique and its variations. Some of the techniques include tapping on certain acupuncture points in order to get the energy to change. Others depend on placing our hands on certain energy centers. Some are based on alternative eye movements. Others focus on developing alternative perceptions of what is happening.

When we successfully change our emotional state in relation to specific stimuli, we also change how we react emotionally, chemically, hormonally, and electronically to that specific situation. This means that our hypothalamus excretes different peptides and our brain creates new synapses in relation to the same stimulus that, until now, was disturbing to us. When this is done a number of times, this new, more positive perception and reaction becomes our new norm.

How do we employ EFT?

In this section we will give only the bare basics concerning how to do EFT. If you would like more information, we recommend the book *Free to Be Happy with Energy Psychology* and the sites www.emofree.com or www.holisticharmony.com/eft/.

Step 1. The Setup

a. We **bring to mind the emotion or physical problem** we want to free ourselves from.

b. We **estimate the SUD,** or subjective units of discomfort (or disturbance), to be from 0 to 10, where zero means no discomfort, emotion, or pain whatsoever and ten means the highest we can imagine.

c. Now we **correct** for **"psychological reversal,"** or resistance to feeling better, just in case it is present, by tapping **on the side of the hand** at the point of the hand with which we would hit a piece of wood if we were performing a karate chop.

1. We tap on the side of the hand while repeating three times the phrase "Even though I have this (fill in your emotion or physical problem), I deeply and profoundly love and accept myself."

2. Then we tap on the **side of the other hand** repeating three times "I choose to be free from this (fill in your emotion or physical problem). You can also use in place of the word "choose," the words "want," "agree," "deserve," or "accept."—Still another option is "It is to my benefit to be free from (fill in your emotion or physical problem).

Step 2: The Tapping Sequence

We are now ready to **tap on the eight points** so as to remove the disturbance in the energy field.

These points are usually the beginning or end points of the acupuncture meridians (energy channels) and can be seen on the accompanying diagram. We tap on them several times each in this sequence. It really does not matter how many times you tap, but it should be more than five.

This initiates the flow of energy through these energy channels, thus correcting the disturbance in the energy field associated with that problem. The tapping should be at a good pace—not too slow—and have an abrupt percussive hit on each tap. never be too hard, though, or painful or in any way damaging.

Except for the point on the top of the head, where we tap with all the fingers of both hands, we tap with the tips of the index and middle finger of each hand. The area covered by these two fingers is larger than the area of the points themselves and helps ensure we hit the point when we tap. We have modified the process and tap with both hands on the same points symmetrically placed on the right and left side of the body. This can be done with alternating tapping, which stimulates the right and left hemispheres of the brain as we tap. This alternating stimulation is also very useful in changing the energy field and, in a way, combines the methods of EFT and EMDR.

Reminder Phrase

As we tap at each point, we can verbally—or perhaps mentally in cases where we do not want to be heard—repeat the reminder phrase. The reminder phrase is simply a declaration of which emotional energy field we are tapping on. This helps us to be focused on this particular energy field as we tap, correcting it with our tapping. The reminder phrase will therefore mention the emotion, physical problem, or desire we are tapping for and perhaps also the stimulus behind it.

Examples:

Fear of heights

Fear of speaking in front of others

Fear of being abandoned

Fear of not having enough money

Fear of being attacked

Fear of old age

Fear of failure

Fear of losing a loved one

Fear of losing a job

Anger when people correct me

Pain in the lower back

Anxiety about this test

The points

Refer to the accompanying diagram to see where the points are located. We have also included, for those interested, the acupuncture meridians and the numbers of the points where we tap. It is not necessary to know or understand these in order to use this process.

In our modified version, we usually tap in this sequence:

1. **Top of the head** (governing vessel, point 20) and on the line connecting the top of the head with the center of the forehead. This is done with all the fingers so that the acupuncture points on the ends of the fingers and thumbs are also stimulated by this process.

On the rest of the points, we tap with the index and middle fingers of each hand.

2. **The corner of the eyebrow** where it unites with the bridge of the nose—referred to as EB, eyebrow point (bladder meridian 2).

3. The **side of the eye** on the temple—referred to as SE, side of eye (gall bladder 1). Here we can also tap toward the back and behind the ears.

4. **Under the eye** at the upper part of the cheek bone—referred to as UE, under eye (stomach meridian 2).

*5a. **Under the nose** and above the lip—referred to as UN, under nose (governing vessel meridian 25–26).

*5b. **Under the lower lip** and above the chin—referred to as CH, chin (conception vessel meridian 24).

6. **Under the armpit** on the side of the body approximately level with the nipples—referred to as UA, under arm (spleen meridian 21).

7. **Under the collarbone** and directly to the left and right of the sternum. This is in the soft spot just below the collarbone (the highest horizontal bone on the front of the body) and to the side of the sternum (the vertical bone in the center of the chest)—referred to as CB, collarbone point (kidney meridian 27).

8. **On the side of the hand** where you would hit a piece of wood if doing a karate chop—referred to as KC, karate chop point (small intestine meridian 3–4). This is the same point we tapped on while correcting for psychological reversal.

Except for the points above and below the lips, all the points are located on the right and left sides of the body (even the collarbone and top of the head points). We suggest that you alternate tapping on the right and left. The following points at the ends of the fingers are stimulated when tapping on the top of the head with all the fingers. If , however, you prefer, you can tap on them separately.

a. **On the outside of the thumb** at the point where the nail unites with the skin. (If you place your palms on your abdomen, the part you tap on will be turned up toward your head,) This is referred to as Th, thumb point (lung meridian 11).

b. **On the outside of the index finger** at the point where the nail unites with the skin. (If you place your palms on your abdomen, the part you tap on will be turned up toward your head,) This is referred to as IF, index finger (large intestine meridian 1).

---

*When tapping on these two points, one hand can be above the lips and the other below.

    c. On the outside of the middle finger at the point where the nail unites with the skin. (If you place your palms on your abdomen, the part you tap on will be turned up toward your head.) This is referred to as MF, middle finger (circulation—sex meridian 9).

    d. On the outside of the little finger at the point where the nail unites with the skin. (If you place your palms on your abdomen, the part you tap on will be turned up toward your head.) This is referred to as BF, baby finger (heart meridian 9).

We do this process of tapping from the top of the head down to the karate point three times as we focus on the emotion.

Evaluating the SUD

We now focus on the thought, emotion, desire, or physical problem that was disturbing us and evaluate where our SUD (our degree of disturbance) is.

We seek to determine whether it has

    a. Risen? (It can sometimes, but this is seldom)

    b. Stayed the same?

    c. Dropped? (Which means we feel less disturbed when we focus on this)

When the SUD does *not* go down

If it has risen or stayed the same, then we perform the next round exactly as we did the previous one. Having now measured our present SUD, we perform the following

    1. The set up—rubbing or tapping with the appropriate corrective phrases for possible psychological reversal. (This is even more important now because, as the discomfort has not subsided at all, there is a greater possibility of the presence of psychological reversal.)

    2. The sequence—tapping the twelve points repeating the reminder phrase.

Having done a second round, we then evaluate again. If the disturbance still has not come down—which is rare—we do exactly the same again.

If we are not getting results, then we need to seek to understand why. Refer to the sources mentioned above or consult an EFT practitioner for help.

When the SUD *does* come down

When the SUD comes down, even just a bit, we alter the process slightly.

1. In the setup while rubbing the sore spot or tapping the side of the hand, we now refer to the problem as "remaining _____."

For example the phrase might be "Even though I have this remaining fear of heights (spiders, snakes, darkness, elevators—whatever it might be), I deeply and profoundly love myself."

or

"Even though I have this remaining pain in my lower back, I deeply and profoundly love myself."

The word "remaining" here is important because it allows our tapping to address the specific energy field that is remaining. Also it psychologically reminds us that the discomfort is already less and is still decreasing.

2. In the step 2 sequence, while tapping on the twelve points, we also refer to "remaining _____."

Examples:

Remaining fear of heights

Remaining fear of elevators

Remaining anger

Remaining lower back pain

At this point we complete our round and check the SUD again. Whether it has gone down or not, we continue with the setup and reminder phrases that refer to the "remaining _____."

We can repeat stages 1 and 2 as many times as we need to until the emotion or physical problem has been seriously reduce or eliminated. Once we have reduced the emotion or physical problem, we then move on to the balancing process.

Step 3: The Balancing Process

This is the strangest part of the procedure. Some people feel silly when they first perform it; however, it plays the role of balancing the energies and the activity of the right and left hemispheres of the brain between tapping sequences.

We tap on the groove created by the bones leading from the wrist to the knuckles of the smallest two fingers (ring finger and little finger). The tapping is done in the groove toward the knuckles. (thyroid 3).

As we tap at a rate of around three to five times a second, we make the following movements.

1. Keeping the head straight, we **look hard down right.**

2. Keeping the head straight, we **look hard down left**.

3. Keeping the head straight, we make **circles** with the eyes to the **right**.

4. Keeping the head straight, we make **circles** with the eyes to the **left**.

5. We **hum** a few bars of any song (Many like "Happy Birthday") for two to five seconds.

6. We **count** from one to five out loud (unless you do not want to be heard).

7. We **hum** a few bars of any tune again. (Two to five seconds).

This may seem silly, but it does help to balance the energies. When we hum and count and hum, we activate the two hemispheres of the brain.

By following this, most people will become free from their specific problem in one to five rounds. If you do not, consult the sources below.

Step 4: Once we have diminished the disturbance and balanced the energy, we are ready to "install" the positive perception, idea, or belief that frees us from that particular emotion. Some of these alternative perceptions are discussed in this book. We choose the new positive idea that we want to strengthen and then repeat stage two, tapping on all the same points in the same way, while having in mind the stimulus. This time, at each point as we tap, we repeat to ourselves (verbally or mentally) the new belief or perception. Focus on feeling and believing what you are repeating. We continue this until we are able to bring to mind the original stimulus and still remain in touch with the new belief.

Step 5: Once we have succeeded in this, we can balance the energy once again as described in stage 3.

Step 6: We can now employ any method of altering our state of mind, such as Freeze Frame, Sedona, Ho'oponopono, or deep relaxation with positive thoughts and projections. (All are described in this book).

Here are some web addresses for further investigation of these methods:

Energy psychology in general – http://www.HolisticHarmony.com/ seminars/ and http://www.holisticharmony.com/eft/index.asp

TFT – Thought Field Therapy – http://www.tftrx.com/callahan.html

EFT – Emotional Freedom Techniques – http://www.emofree.com

BSFF – Be Set Free Fast – http://www.besetfreefast.com/

TAT – Tapas Acupressure Technique – http://www.tatlife.com/

EMDR – Eye Movement Desensitization and Reprocessing

WHEE – Wholistic Hybrid of EFT and EMDR –

http://www.wholistichealingresearch.com/selfhealingwheeandother. html

Sedona Method (from Lester Levenston and Hale Dwoskin) – http:// www.sedona.com/

Freeze Frame (from the Institute of HeartMath) – http://www .heartmath.org/

Ho'oponopono (from the Spiritual teachers of Hawaii) – (http://www .hooponoponotheamericas.org/index.htm)

CHAPTER SIX

The Twelve-Step
Manifestation Process

Many of you will have read the book or seen the movie entitled *The Secret*. Actually, what is taught is not a secret. It has been known for thousands of years by all religions and philosophical and spiritual groups, that our beliefs, thoughts, and emotions create our reality.

We have discussed in previous chapters the laws of attraction, mirroring, and sympathetic vibration, through which we manifest our personal, social, and planetary reality. So how can we methodically create for ourselves, our families, society, and the planet the most abundant and satisfying reality possible? Here is a basic summary of the method of attraction, or manifestation.

The Preparation

1. **Gratitude for our present abundance.** The first step is to realize, as already mentioned, that we have already created a reality considerably more positive than 85 percent of our fellow souls on this planet. To better realize this, we can make a list of all that we can feel grateful for. Be sure to include as many family members as possible. Also remember some things that we often take for granted, such as shelter from the elements, clothing, food, electricity, music, dance, nature, clean running water, heat, hot water, and the freedom to move about without restrictions. Include any appliances or machines that add comfort, effectiveness, or creativity to our lives, including a car or computer. Remember that knowledge and education are not to be taken for granted. They, too, are gifts from the universe we can feel grateful for. Many cannot take for granted eyesight, hearing, the ability to walk, or use of their hands.

Take time to make your list now. Once you have done so, continue.

2. Realizing how much you already have leads to a number of other realizations and feelings such as the following:

   a. Feeling lucky or **blessed and loved** by the Divine or the universe, which has given you all of what billions of your fellow souls have not been given.

   b. The **power of creation and manifestation**. This is also a list of what you already created. Just as we need to take responsibility for creating whatever is not satisfying in our lives, we also need to realize that we have co-created with the Divine all that we feel grateful for.

   c. Feeling loved, blessed, powerful, and able to manifest in co-operation with the Divine or the universe, we are now in a much more **positive and confident position** to make the adjustments and improvements in our reality that we seek.

3. Now make a list of what you would like to change in your reality, including

   a. What you would like to improve, such as health, abundance, or relationships.

   b. What you would like to create anew, such as a projects or goals for yourself or for others.

   c. What you would like to alter, such as stopping smoking or eating less food

   d. How you would like to be, such as more self-confident, more loving toward others and yourself, freer from fears or selfishness or the ego.

   e. Enlightenment, self-actualization.

4. Choose one to three of the most important goals from your list to work on manifesting.

The Twelve-Step Manifestation Process

Now you need to align yourself with what you want to attract or manifest.

1. Read your gratitude list daily for at least thirty days—preferably in the morning when you wake, in the evening before you sleep, or both. See if you can add something new to this list each day.

2. Make signs stating that your present goal(s) have *already* been achieved—in the present tense. Place these signs in various locations where you will see them often throughout the day.

3. Do the following mental exercise daily one or more times:

   a. **Relax** the body and mind by **breathing** slowly and deeply as you allow all of the muscles and the mind to relax. Imagine that you are inhaling peace and exhaling tension and tiredness.

   b. Then allow your **attention to flow from the bottom of your feet to the top of your head;** allow all the muscles to relax as you do.

   c. Then **count down from 10 to 1,** relaxing more and more deeply with each count.

   d. Now **bring to mind all that you already have and feel grateful for**. Feel gratitude, happiness, and peace for all that you have.

   e. **Feel loved and blessed** by the universe.

   f. Now **visualize that your desired reality has already manifested**—that you have exactly what you want, that you are as you would like to be, and that your life is already as you would like it to be. Spend time feeling gratitude and happiness that your new reality has already manifested. Experience this newly created reality as strongly as possible, visualizing as many details as possible along with all of the positive emotions that you **now feel** because what you desire has become reality.

   g. Spend some time **allowing a spiritual light to fill your body and mind,** removing any aspects of your subconscious that might resist this positive change in your life. Allow the divine to remove all inner obstacles to the manifestation of what is for your highest benefit.

h. Now spend a **little more time visualizing your new life** with your goal already achieved, dwelling on how you feel and how your attitudes and behaviors have changed since you now have what you want or need.

i. Be sure to **visualize only the end result** of what you want to manifest and not limit yourself by imagining how it will happen or (even worse) how you *cannot* imagine how it can happen. Allow the universe to manage the how. Just let go of the how and trust that the universe knows the most appropriate way for you. Imagine only the end result.

4. Throughout the day, without necessarily going through all of this process, bring the image and feelings of having already created your desired reality to mind frequently. Do this whenever you feel fearful, helpless, or discouraged. Do not allow the mind to focus on negative feelings, but rather bring to mind the feeling of already having what you need and want. On the other hand do not fear, fight, or become angry at your negative thoughts or feelings. Simply accept that they are a product of your old unenlightened programming that you received from a society that is still in the process of evolution and is limited by many false beliefs. Then simply move your attention to the feeling that what you want has already become a reality and feel all the positive feelings that accompany that thought.

5. You can increase your alignment with your "under construction" or "in the oven" reality by writing a detailed description of what it is like, how you feel, and what has now changed in yourself and your life now that what you have wanted for so long has actually become a reality. All of this must be described as a present reality, not a future one. Focus on feelings. Read this, too, every day for at least thirty days. You can also rewrite it daily or as often as you like, expressing it each time as it comes to you. Reading aligns you to this reality, but writing aligns you even more.

6. Start doing now what you believe you will do when your desired reality is "completely constructed" or is "fully baked." Check out your written or mental description and see how you imagine your thinking, behavior, habits, and actions will change when you have your new reality. Consider making those changes now. When you act now as you imagine you will act when you have what you want, that aligns you deeply with that manifestation. Think creatively. For, example if you feel that you would help others economically if you had more money, then do so now, within your means. By giving to others, you are aligning yourself with the abundance of the universe.

7. Give what you would like to receive. In general we can manifest much more easily when we give what we want to receive or attract. If you would like more money, give some. If you would like more love, affection, attention, acceptance, caring, respect, or support, then give them all and you will eventually receive what you give. Some may say, "But I have been giving all my life and not receiving. I am the victim, the abused." Many may feel this way, but if they investigate themselves deeply, they will realize that at some level they were also seeking to receive and that their giving was not totally free from needing. Also they might discover that they have subconscious resistance to receiving what they consciously desire and need. This, however, is a subject for another chapter or book. For now suffice it to say that giving what we want in order to attract is another way of aligning ourselves with what we seek to manifest.

8. Create a vision board where you pin or paste images, photos, cuttings, drawings, objects, and texts that represent your goal and connect you to it visually. Place this where you can see it frequently. Spending time creating this visual representation connects you to your goal and aligns you to it energetically as do the above-mentioned steps.

9. Wish and work for the good of the whole. Seek to help others in every way that you can. This aligns you with the power of the universe, which protects and supports those who care for and work for the whole. The main lesson of these testing times is to choose love and unity rather than continue in the path of separateness, selfishness, and alienation that created this crisis.

At this stage in our evolutionary process the time has come to perceive all as members of our family and seek goals that benefit all—not only ourselves and our family. We may reflect on whether or not our goals are actually the highest ones we can conceive of, whether they are really good for us physically, mentally, emotionally, and spiritually. What is really good for us on all levels is always also good for the whole.

10. Speak and express yourself positively. Do not talk about what you do not like or want. Talking and emoting about we do not want only aligns us with exactly what we do not want. Do not talk about health, economic, work, or relationship problems. Do not talk about fears, guilt, or other negative emotions, as you simply amplify them. Speak about what you like and enjoy and appreciate. This will bring more of that into your life.

Clarification: It is fine to speak about what is bothering you with someone who is able to professionally help you create another reality, such as a doctor, psychologist, economic advisor, or relationship counselor. These professionals will help you take responsibility for your present creation and support you in manifesting the reality you desire. This is totally different from talking with your friends and relatives about your problems and getting their attention for your problems. This will only crystallize your present reality even further.

11. Take actions toward the manifestation of your goals. Even though you are leaving the how to the universe, there are always actions you can take in the present toward creating what you need. You may take classes or otherwise learn what you need to know. You may need to let go of something old in order to receive something new. You may want to let go of attachments that are sapping energy, money, or time from your real goals at this time. You may want to ask for support from someone who can help you.

12. Remove all inner obstacles toward manifesting your desired reality. You may need to let go of some fears, feelings, of unworthiness, victimization, helplessness, or other—perhaps subconscious obstacles—that may be obstructing your new creation. This subconscious self-sabotage is also called "psychological reversal." While we may consciously desire something very

much, we may also subconsciously fear its manifestation or, alternatively, fear that we are not worthy of it or that we are unlucky and can never have it. In such a case, we will be emitting, along with our positive images, thoughts, and feelings, these subconscious result-canceling feelings and beliefs.

Suffice it to say here that we need to remove these inner obstacles in order to create our consciously desired reality. The most effective means for doing this are the various forms of energy psychology such as EFT, TAT, BSFF, TFT, EMDR, the Sedona Method, and Ho'oponopono, which we will discuss later. You can also find introductory information about these at http://www.HolisticHarmony.com/seminars.

This combination of dissolving inner obstacles and visualizing and aligning ourselves with our desired goal is a fool-proof method of success. All of this is explained in much more detail in my book, *Twenty-Five Ways to Manifest Your Ideal Reality.*

A word about soul decisions

Some people wonder, "what if I am not supposed to have that," or "what if God or my higher self does not want me to have that? What if I have a karmic obstruction toward the manifestation of that goal?" Or they may think, "isn't it better just to let God decide what I should have? Maybe I shouldn't really ask for anything?"

We are divine beings who have projected our consciousness into these temporary bodies and minds. We are actually divine and worthy of all the good of this world. We are, in fact, creating our reality in cooperation with the Divine and our fellow beings. We are here to learn to create ever more positive realities that simulate the harmony, abundance, and love that characterize our true selves.

There is absolutely no reason why we do not deserve a wonderful and abundant reality. There is also no reason why "God" might not want us to have all that we desire. Christ spoke about this when he said, "What Father would give stones to his children who are asking for food?" And, "Why bother about tomorrow when God will give you everything you need as long as you live according to his laws." (This means the laws of love and unity.)

The only obstacles to our manifesting something that we desire are those we as souls chose before our birth and even during our lives. As souls we may have chosen to learn certain inner lessons by not being able to satisfy some needs externally. If, in fact, as souls we have made such a decision, we may actually internally obstruct the manifestation of a goal until we can learn to feel security, self-worth, freedom, happiness, and love for others and ourselves without that which we believe we must have. In other words, we need to let go of our attachment to, and dependence on, what we are seeking to create before we can create it.

I know that this is confusing because we have already mentioned that experiencing positive feelings about what we seek to manifest is essential to attracting it. This is true. But if we are also experiencing fear that we will not be able to create what we want or fear that we cannot be well until we do, this is a self-canceling energy that may obstruct what we want to manifest. This would be the case if we have made a soul decision to overcome the illusion that our self-worth, security, and happiness are actually dependent on whether or not we get what we want. When we are attached in this way, we experience a wide variety of negative emotions such as the following:

1. Fear that we will not be able to get what we want.

2. Fear that even if we have it, we might lose it or someone might take it from us.

3. Failure, self-rejection, shame, and helplessness if we do not create it.

4. Jealousy and envy of those who have what we want

5. Anger and hate toward those we consider to be the cause of our not getting what we want.

We need to understand that above and beyond all that we seek to create, our ultimate life purpose is to realize our own inner self-worth, security, peace, freedom, happiness, and fulfillment. What can we possibly gain by having all that we want materially if that only increases the illusion that we cannot be well without it and we never have a chance to experience our true spiritual greatness? All of these external objects and situations will then only serve to increase our ignorance.

Therefore, as strange as it might seem, we can manifest much more easily what we would love to enjoy when we also know that we can be worthy, safe, and happy without it. For example, if you have chosen to learn to experience your own self-worth without external affirmation, acceptance, or love, then you may have set up spiritual agreements with those souls who are playing the roles of your family or other close ones to withhold such affirmation until you learn this lesson so that you can realize your own self-worth and be free from the need for external verification.

Those who have made such a soul decision will have placed an obstacle to receiving external affirmation until they no longer need it in order to love themselves and others and live happy and creative lives. Once this lesson has been learned, the obstruction can be removed—especially with Ho'oponopono—and they can receive unlimited love, affirmation, and even admiration because they are not dependent on it any more. It is no longer an obstacle to their evolutionary process.

Some may have established a similar obstruction concerning money or material abundance or perhaps concerning support from others. Our soul decision (not God's will for us, but our own will for us) may be to live without money until we can feel secure, peaceful, worthy, and happy without it. Once we have learned that, the obstacle is removed.

The solution then is to upgrade all attachments and addictions that are characterized by fear of not getting, or of losing, what we need to *preferences*. A preference is something we want and give our energy to creating with the knowledge that we are, and can be, well without it. We choose to be with someone because we love and enjoy them, not because we have the illusion that we cannot feel worthy, secure, or happy without them. This is an illusion. How can the other six billion souls on this earth be fine without this person we believe we cannot be well without?

Not all souls have made such soul decisions and thus may not have inner resistance to manifesting what they want. Some say that such soul contracts can also be removed by asking that they be, but the most effective means for moving past them is to learn the lessons that we set them there to learn. Thus we need to experience our own inner power, security, self-worth, happiness, and fulfillment while we simultaneously visualize our preferred reality and experience all of the positive emotions we have now that it has become our new reality. In this way, we have many positive emotions about our new reality without any of the fears that are created by attachment, which is a negation of what we truly are.

The techniques of energy psychology are very effective for letting go of the fears created by attachment, as are Ho'oponopono, meditation, and the study of and employment of spiritual truths.

The Field of All Possibilities

All of creation comes forth from the "quantum field," or the "field of pure consciousness," "the implicit order," according to David Bohm, or the "field of pure potential," as expressed by Deepak Chopra. All that exists comes forth from pure consciousness, which forms into energy and then becomes matter and its various interactions.

We can understand this with the example of our television or a movie projector. All the images on the TV screen are temporary formations of the one white formless light that remains on the screen even when no signals are forming it into temporary images. All images including the "good" and "bad," the "peaceful" and "violent" are simply mutations of that one formless light.

In the same way, all of the universe is a manifestation of the one universal consciousness that we compose. Nothing exists that it not a manifestation of that one consciousness, which is actually our true self. It is natural and logical then, that, if we are able to experience that formless aspect of ourselves, we will be in touch with the source of all the realities we seek to create—as they come from the same formless source.

Although this deserves a long and detailed explanation, we can just say here that we can enhance our creative power by daily experiencing that formless and thought-free part of our existence. This is usually done through meditation, where we allow our thoughts to slow down, perhaps by focusing on our breathing or some positive archetype or value. We then learn to focus on the space or emptiness between our thoughts. We might become aware of the silence, however small it might be, that is there when one thought has ended and before the next one comes into our mind. With practice, we can learn to expand that space and experience pure consciousness without thoughts.

This is the space from which all becomes manifest. When we visualize what we seek to manifest from this state, our thought power is much greater. Imagine the difference between painting upon a canvas that is already painted on and one that is blank. Rather than visualizing our preferred reality projected on an old limited thought pattern, we learn to visualize our reality onto pure consciousness, which has no preexisting states or limits.

A New Definition of Abundance

We need to expand out perception of abundance. Most people measure their abundance exclusively by how much money and how many possessions they have. These may to some degree contribute to our abundance, but equally important are health, loving relationships, friendships, knowledge, meaningful work, human values, techniques, freedom of belief, and expression, nature, music, dance, and so many other aspects of our lives that make life abundant, meaningful, and fulfilling.

Cultivate Happiness

Arrange your life so that you have ample opportunities to enjoy peaceful and happy moments. Leave time and space to laugh, sing, dance, and share with loved ones. Specify times of sharing and enjoying things with your family and friends. This could mean eating together, singing, dancing, telling jokes and stories, watching comedies on TV, walking in nature, swimming, shopping, or going out together.

You can also enjoy time alone reading, listening to music, resting, walking, meditating, exercising, praying, painting, writing, working in the garden, or any other enjoyable or creative activity that appeals to you.

There is no reason why we cannot enjoy ourselves during testing times and laugh and be as happy as any other time. That is part of our lesson— to be happy in all situations. Happiness will then become a habit, and we will attract much more from the universe than we will with sadness, anxiety, bitterness, or fear.

Please go over the twelve-step manifestation process and employ it now for what you would like to manifest in your life.

All of these techniques are explained in much more detail in the book *Twenty-Five Ways to Manifest Your Ideal Life* (http://www.HolsiticHarmony.com).

CHAPTER SEVEN

Ho'oponopono and How to Transform Our Reality by Purifying Ourselves

The ancient Hawaiian healing technique called Ho'oponopono asks us to take 100 percent responsibility for whatever appears in our reality—for whatever we perceive or comes to our attention. In this process we cleanse ourselves and our personal input into what we call, "our reality," which is personal, communal, and planetary. We change the world by changing ourselves. It is both a method for solving problems and for healing ourselves and others (as well as situations). It is also a means for spiritual development and enlightenment.

Here we will present a short explanation. You can find more details at http://www.HolisticHarmony.com/archives/capsules/hopono.asp.

The process is simple:

1. We **realize or remember** that whatever we are observing or whatever is affecting us in any way is there because it is **reflecting something within ourselves**—mainly our personal memories, beliefs, emotions, and programming. We are attracting that specific reality because it is time to clean a certain part of ourselves that is contributing to it and actually co-creating it in some way. The specific reality might be persons or situations that seem to be not well—not harmonious. Or it could be something that bothers us personally, such as someone's behavior or a world situation.

2. Having taken responsibility for the reality before us, we now ~~we ask~~ that person, situation, or attribute for **forgiveness for our participation** in that specific reality that has come into our awareness. Instead of asking for forgiveness, we can simply acknowledge that we are participants in creating this reality. Another option is to thank the person or situation for the opportunity it has offered for self-knowledge and growth.

43

Note: It is highly unlikely that we will understand what our contribution to this is. It could be from our deep subconscious or even deeper dimensions of ourselves that we are not aware of. The cause within us may be as simple as the fact that we are unable to perceive the Divine in ourselves or others, or in what is happening, and thus are allowing whatever it is to annoy us.

3. We then **feel and express our love** to whatever was bothering us or seems to be not well or harmonious. When doing so, we seek to feel acceptance, love, unity, and good wishes for that person, event, or situation.

4. We then need to **feel love and acceptance toward ourselves** as we are and let go of any guilt or self-condemnation with regards to this or any other reason.

5. Then we **release the person, situation, or event**—whatever is bothering us—from the need to be that way any more for our evolutionary process. We give it permission to change.

6. Then we **thank the Divine** for **dissolving these unenlightened memories**, tendencies, fears, and beliefs into the light of pure divine consciousness—which is actually their original state.

If possible, we can then remain some time in a state of emptiness or inner light as we allow the Divine to cleanse us of anything that might be attracting this undesired reality.

One Hundred Percent Responsibility?

This concept of responsibility is quite difficult for most of us to digest. Can we take responsibility for other people's irresponsible or unethical actions? How can we be responsible for those who are abusing women and children or killing innocent persons in Iraq, Africa, or elsewhere? Can we take responsibility for terrorist acts around the world? Such reactions naturally come to mind when we are asked to believe and employ this revolutionary system.

How can we be responsible for what "we" have not done and for what we would "probably" (we will never know until we find ourselves in the same circumstances) never do? How can we be responsible for what others are doing on the other side of the world and for situations perpetuated by leaders that we never voted for, do not agree with, and even condemn?

Also how do we reconcile this truth with another equally obvious and valid truth that each of us is the exclusive creator of his or her reality and that others do not create our reality and we do not create theirs. These truths seem to be irreconcilable, yet, millions have found Ho'oponopono to be a really superb technique that leads ultimately to purity, love, and freedom from negativity. Even more impressively, it actually does change the external world. Let us play with ideas that may help us understand how it works.

Our Collective Unconscious

We have many common emotions, beliefs, and modes of functioning, as hypothesized by Carl Jung in his theory of the collective unconscious. We share many programmings, fears, emotions, and desires. It may just be that we are all affected by each other's subconscious. Many experiments today show that we can be affected by what others are feeling, even though consciously we are not aware of what is happening. This is especially true of people with whom we are closely bound emotionally.

Quantum physics has shown that the same is true of particles that have been in contact at some point in their history. Whatever happens to the one immediately affects the other.

Psychologists are also aware of the "connected container effect," which speculates that people are like two containers with water connected by a pipe at their base. When we suppress the water in one container, it will rise in the other. It is well know that in a marital or family situation, one person's suppressed emotions are communicated and often expressed by other members. Whatever we do to our own "water system" will affect the others who are connected to us in this way. We are affecting others by our invisible emotional connections to them.

Social paradigms

We are also affected by and participate in the common social paradigms into which we were born and raised. When we accept and act according to these paradigms, we are augmenting them for everyone else. Thus we are supporting others' belief systems by allowing ourselves to be limited by those belief systems. If we believe that those who are different from us (in race, religion, social class) are a danger to us, then we are co-creating that reality. If we believe there is not enough for all of us, we are co-creating that reality. If we believe that life is difficult and people are not to be trusted, we are contributing to those realities.

Our Common Morphogenetic Field

Biologist Rupert Sheldrake's theory of the morphogenetic field adds a biological dimension to this. He believes that our bodies and minds get their information from a common pool of knowledge and tendencies that exist in a field commonly accessible to us all. When any one of us makes a change in lifestyle, emotions, or ways of thinking, those changes to some degree affect the state of our commonly shared field, and that makes this new way of thinking or reacting more available to all others sharing that field. This works for all emotions, beliefs, and behaviors, negative and positive. Remaining in our old unenlightened beliefs and behaviors affects all others through this shared field. We are co-responsible for what is happening. On the other hand, our positive changes enable others to do the same.

Our Personal Causal Body

Philosophical systems teach that we each have a personal "causal body," where all of our soul memories and tendencies, qualities and abilities are stored along with all of our fears and other emotions. In short, all of our positive and negative tendencies are stored there. Upon birth these dictate the type of physical body we will have as well as the conditions of our birth and our emotional and mental tendencies. These affect, but do not exclusively determine, most major events of our lives. We are attracting realities that, to a great degree, are formed by the content of our causal body. This does not, however, create an ironclad fate because in each moment we are adding and removing qualities from that causal field when we change the way we perceive, think, act, and react.

When we perform Ho'oponopono and other perception- and reaction-altering methods, we changing the content of our conscious and subconscious minds as well as our causal body. We are requesting and allowing for all tendencies in our causal bodies that might be contributing to what we are perceiving and being affected by to be removed and dissolved once again into pure consciousness—which is what they ultimately are.

Universal Consciousness

All thoughts, emotions, memories, actions, and reactions—as well as all physical objects and beings and the interactions between them—are simply manifestations of one universal consciousness. This is similar to the fact that all images on the movie or TV screen are temporary manifestations of one white light that only temporarily takes these forms—including the "good," "bad," loving, hateful, mineral, plant, animal, human, and all interactions between them.

The white light of the TV, when nothing is playing, is the like the zero point from which all appears and dissolves. In Ho'oponopono, we are asking the Divine to dissolve all tendencies that might be contributing to what we are witnessing back into their real nature, which is white, undifferentiated light.

Our Common Causal Body

Similar to the morphogenetic field, we all share a common universal causal body. There is a causal body for each species of animals and plant and one for all men and one for all women and one for all humans and one for the planet itself.

This common causal body includes all of our shared tendencies that affect humanity and the planet as a whole. Thus, when we get free from anger, fear, or guilt, we make those tendencies less available in the shared causal body. Love, understanding, responsibility, and peace then become more available.

Ho'oponopono and all forms of energy psychology such as EFT, TAT, TFT, BSFF, EMDR, the Sedona Method, Freeze Frame, meditation, prayer, and wide variety of other methods allow us to perceive and react differently. When these old memories and programmings dissolve, they are also lessened in all of humanity as a whole.

Spiritual Teachings

All religions teach the concept of divine justice. Everyone is getting exactly what they justly deserve based on what they have done in the past until now. In Christianity this is expressed in Christ's words, "as you sow, so shall you reap," and "as you judge, so will you be judged." Also when Christ healed the paralyzed man, he said to him, "get up and walk—your sins have been forgiven," indicating that he was paralyzed because of some past mistakes.

According to these spiritual teachings and the law of karma taught by eastern religions, someone could harm us only if the universal laws of perfect justice allow them to. Thus, if the universe is allowing someone to behave in negative ways, our conclusion can only be that, even though this feels totally unjust and wrong, it is being allowed and there must therefore be some hidden justice— some "cause" within me that is attracting or allowing this.

The actual meaning of Ho'oponopono is "to correct or make right again." We simply assume that we, in this or perhaps (if you believe so) in some past life, have done something that is contributing to what is occurring. Another possibility is that it is happening because we need to learn something, in which case we can express our gratitude and love to the other for giving us this opportunity to learn and grow through this experience.

The next question is, how do we affect each other and how is our personal and collective reality created?

Creating Reality through Interpretation and Projection

We create our subjective reality by the way in which we interpret behaviors, situations, and events. Unfortunately most often we are *not* perceiving what is there, but actually perceiving what we have been programmed to *believe* is there. Our belief system works as a filter that subjectively and selectively interprets whatever we perceive in ways that corroborate what we already believe and ignores what we do not.

For example, if we believe that others will reject us and do not love us, we will interpret their suggestions or other actions as a form of rejection and lack of love for us even when that is simply not the truth. We have all been surprised to discover that people have misinterpreted our actions, believing that we had motives and feelings that we never had. We do the same. We project onto persons and situations motives and dangers that simply are not there. When we do so, we experience fear, pain, and bitterness, creating unnecessary unhappiness for ourselves and others.

Conflicting Belief Systems and Memories

We could subdivide our beliefs into the following categories:

1. Emotionally Charged Impressions – These are not so much beliefs as impressions that are imprinted on the mind during traumatic experiences. The mind then identifies this particular stimulus with an emotionally charged feeling, and when we think

of it, we feel fear and other emotions. This kind of "belief" has a strong emotional charge but is not based on observations and facts. Rather, it is based on one or two intense experiences, which are not representative of reality as a whole.

2. Mistaken Childhood Conclusions – These are mistaken beliefs about reality in which we perceive ourselves as weak, wrong, unlovable, and culpable for just about everything that happens around us, such as our parents' and others' anger, absence, unhappiness, indifference, divorce, illness, and even death. We falsely interpret that we are unworthy or incapable and that others will always behave toward us in ways similar to what we experienced in childhood.

These first two categories are usually repressed in the subconscious mind (in the shadow, or inner child) because of the pain and confusion they produce. We suppress them so that we can focus and function in our daily lives.

Although these beliefs are repressed so that we do not feel the unpleasant negative emotional energy charge associated with them, they are activated whenever we come into contact with, or think of, a specific stimulus. They generate fear, panic, emotional withdrawal, and often aggressive behavior. They also create psychosomatic illnesses. They control our reactions to events, situations, and persons. Most importantly, they *attract* the realities we encounter.

Because of their repression and subsequent isolation from our conscious mind, these first two belief systems do not evolve as we do. They remain in their original state regardless of our evolving logic, improved reasoning, new experiences, and spiritual faith. Unless we engage in inner psychological or spiritual work, they receive no new data.

3. Our Evolving Conscious Belief System – This is our conscious belief system that, as it processes new data, reevaluates its perceptions of reality, seeking to make the adjustments necessary to understand the truths behind the phenomena we observe. This conscious belief system is evolving in a small number of people. Many have stopped processing new data and thus have remained with the same conscious belief system for many years and will leave their bodies with it.

This belief system understands that we are safe, secure, good, worthy, and capable. It also realizes that we are not in danger from people, heights, cars, insects, dogs, cats, elevators, airplanes, and so on. The facts available to it cause it to realize that its fears are unfounded. It also realizes that our self-worth has nothing to do with what others say, think, or do.

4. Our Spiritual Intuitive Faith – These beliefs are usually based on intuition or faith rather than proof. We *feel* that what we believe is true. In addition to being affected by others' spiritual beliefs, we also experience our own inner awakenings or revelations in which we just "know" that something is true.

According to Ho'oponopono, this divine inspiration can occur only when the mind is purified of the previous three types of mental content, all of which are created and limited by memory.

The reality is that we often experience behaviors, events, and situations through simultaneous beliefs from all four categories, which create conflicting emotions and reactions to what is happening. We might simultaneously feel love, peace, hurt, and anger because our various beliefs are creating different internal realities. Thus, one basic way in which we create our reality is the way in which we interpret whatever is happening in our lives. No two persons create the same reality with the same external stimuli.

Creating Reality through Attraction and Mirroring

The second factor contributing to our personal reality is how we actually attract or create the events that occur in our lives—what actually happens to us.

Of the various theories available, the one that states that we ourselves are the creators of our reality seems to explain a larger, more encompassing portion of the reality we perceive. This explanation becomes even more understandable when we remove the illusion of separation between us as individual expressions of the Divine and divinity itself. When we perceive ourselves as temporary expressions of Divine Consciousness or divine energy in the physical realm, it becomes clear that we are all individually and collectively co-creating our personal and social reality. We are the Divine itself encased in temporary bodies. We are creating and forming our reality. We do so in various ways:

a. The past. Our previous thoughts, actions, choices, feelings, and words all have a causal impact on our present reality. This concept is accepted by all religions and spiritual philosophies. Not all may believe in reincarnation, but all *do* believe in cause and effect, as we have already mentioned. Our choices to care for ourselves or not, to communicate sincerely and honestly or not, to help and love others or not, to free ourselves from fears or not, all have their effect on our present reality.

b. The present. Our present thoughts, beliefs, expectations, fears, guilt, and other emotions and behaviors all create our present reality through the laws of reflection and attraction. Others, and life itself, reflect back to us the content of our mind and behavior on all levels. We attract rejection when we reject ourselves, fear or expect rejection, or reject others. If we think, speak, or act antagonistically or egotistically, we attract the same. Basically, we attract whatever we fear, love, desire, and hate, as well as what we expect and what we do.

Life wisely mirrors back to us our own thoughts, emotions, beliefs, roles, and behaviors, offering us an opportunity to look inward and let go of those aspects of ourselves that are attracting what is unpleasant for us. In such a case, our lesson is to discover what is being reflected and transform it. Otherwise we will continue to attract our present reality. This fact is basic to Ho'oponopono. This is what we need to clean in order to heal what we are co-creating.

It is important to understand that the power and opportunity for positive change is in the present and nowhere else. We cannot change the past, but we can change our perception of the past—and thus its effect upon us in the present. We do not know the future but can form it by our choices in the now.

Some people accept negative realities believing that it is some karma that they have to suffer. There is no benefit from suffering or being punished if we do not learn something from the experience and if it does not initiate change. The concept that we must suffer for past mistakes has no value if that pain does not become an opportunity for growth.

c. Our soul choices. The third factor that determines the nature of the events occurring in our lives are our soul choices. We as souls chose, even before birth, that we would like to, or need to, learn certain lessons as a part of our evolutionary process. If we have chosen to learn self-acceptance, we will make a contract with those close to us to test our ability to feel our self-worth even in the face of disapproval or rejection. If we have decided to learn unconditional love or forgiveness, we will logically choose close contact with persons who will be difficult for us to love. In this way we have the opportunity to overcome our fears and love even those persons. If we would like to learn self-dependency, we will set up a life drama in which we will not easily find support from others. We also have the free will to resist learning any of those lessons.

When we are passing through difficult times, it may not because we have been "bad" in the past, but because we have chosen to learn specific lessons. Through Ho'oponopono we are releasing those persons with whom we have made these contracts from the need to continue playing their roles that test us, because we have learned the lesson, which is to take responsibility for our reality and love them.

Thus, we and all others create our personal and collective reality through our

a. Past beliefs, words, choices, actions, and behaviors.

b. Present beliefs, words, expectations, choices, actions, and behaviors.

c. Our soul decisions to learn certain lessons.

d. How our presently programmed belief systems interpret what is happening.

How Do We Affect Each Other?

Sympathetic vibration is a law of physics that states, among other things, that if we have two guitars or two pianos and we strike a cord on one of them, then the cord on the other that is tuned to the same frequency as the one we have struck will be the most affected and will start to vibrate. A vibration of one will affect the other only if it is tuned to the same frequency. If it is tuned to another frequency, it will likely not be stimulated.

We can imagine in the same way that we are affecting each other by the conscious and subconscious frequencies that we are emitting. We and others would not be affected if we did not have something within ourselves being stimulated by what is happening or being emitted by the other. We will investigate later the possible aspects of our psychology that might be stimulating aspects in others and vice versa.

We supply the stimulus—they create their reality. They supply the stimulus—we create our reality. It is important to clarify that we are responsible only for our conscious and subconscious output in the past and present—but not for what actually happens to the other. That is their creation.

Our only power is to purify our own selves and remove (or ask the Divine to remove) our aspects that affect, or attract through sympathetic vibration, negative realities for ourselves and others. Ho'oponopono is the process of stopping our own strings from vibrating at those frequencies so that we cease adding to others' realities. We are purifying our own input in the reality around us.

We are affected by others in the same way. When others' vibrating strings stimulate movement in us, they are the stimulus, but it is our own programming that causes us to be affected and create our own personal reality.

Quantum Physics—Collapsing the Wave

Quantum physics tells us that a photon or electron is actually a wave of possibilities until there is a witness that causes that wave to collapse into a specific particle in a specific place and time. It appears that the witness causes the wave of possibilities to leave that state of many possibilities and become one specific reality as we know it.

We might imagine that something similar is happening between ourselves and life. Imagine life as a wave of possibilities, all of which exist together in an unmanifest state. In this state nothing is formed yet. All is possible. Memories and programs are not yet limiting this conscious- energy.

Once pure consciousness begins to express itself through our programmed minds, it becomes limited and tends to attract what is in agreement with our memories and programming. Our beliefs and emotions cause the unlimited formless consciousness to form into what we call our reality—with people, actions, and events—all of which are reflections of and responses to our inner content.

Ho'oponopono is a process for cleaning out our inner content so that we can cease distorting the expression of this pure consciousness in our lives. When we ask others to forgive us, it is not because we have done them some harm or made a mistake. It is because we are acknowledging that we ourselves are creating our reality and not them. Also we are realizing that something in our programming has brought them into our awareness and causes us to notice them and perhaps have feelings about what is happening or what they are doing.

Once we realize that it is our own inner reality that is causing this outer reality to manifest and affect us, then we are free from feeling that we are the victims or that others are responsible for our reality. We are taking 100 percent responsibility for our own reality. We realize that the only way to change that reality is to free ourselves from whatever there is within us that is contributing to it—even though we do not know what it might be.

Our Inner Content

Our beliefs, emotions, programmings, needs, desire, fears, attachments, and behaviors all reflect back to us through others' behaviors and through life itself. Following is a list of some aspects of ourselves that might be reflecting back to us through others' behaviors or our current situations.

Note: Ho'oponopono does not require that we know what it is within us that needs to be cleaned.

The presence of any of the below can easily attract corresponding behaviors and situations.

1. When we feel negative emotions about what is happening, we attract them so that we can become free within ourselves.

2. When we have specific limiting beliefs about others and what is happening, or when we perceive someone or something as bad, wrong, unjust, etc., we attract them so that we can work on it.

3. Our own behaviors until now toward this person or toward others in the past reflect back to us in the present so that we can learn from them.

4. Our fears attract and create realities, especially our fears concerning our self-worth, security, freedom, pleasure, or control.

5. We also attract what we expect from others and life.

6. Our doubts limit our reality to what we believe we deserve.

7. How we behave toward ourselves causes others to behave toward us in similar ways.

8. Unresolved childhood experiences tend to replay repeatedly in our lives until we manage to heal them.

9. The roles we identify with for our meaning, self-worth, and security can attract life situations and corresponding behaviors from others so that we can free ourselves from the illusions and limitations of those roles. We might be playing some of the following roles:

A. the victim

B. the intimidator

C. the teacher

D. the parent

E. the child

F. the intelligent one

G. the righteous one

H. the rebel

I. the strong one—without needs

J. the just one

K. the good person

L. the one responsible for all

M. the server

N. the weak one

O. the spiritual person

P. the judge

Q. the aloof one,

R. the critic or interrogator

S. some other role.

10. Those needs and attachments that are limiting our peace, happiness, love, or evolution may reflect in various life situations and behaviors so that we can have an opportunity to free ourselves from them.

11. Our tendency to feel guilty attracts behaviors and situations that stimulate that programming so that we can free ourselves from it.

12. We bring into our lives whatever we criticize, judge, reject, or have prejudiced perceptions of.

13. We attract whatever causes us to feel jealousy, pain, anger, bitterness, injustice, or any other negative emotion so that we can have an opportunity to get free from the illusions that create those emotions.

14. We attract whatever we cannot forgive in others or in ourselves.

15. When we compare ourselves to others, we bring them into our reality.

16. Our own inner conflicts and self-doubt attracts specific behaviors from others that bring those feelings to the surface.

17. When we fail to communicate clearly and assertively, but without criticism or condemnation, we create realities in which we do not get what we need.

18. If we have become accustomed to a reality, we tend to stay in it because of our fear of change.

19. If we fear happiness, abundance, health, being loved, etc., we will obstruct positive realities.

These and other aspects of our inner world can very easily become contributing factors in the realities we are co-creating.

How Might We Be Contributing to World Crises?

Most of us are unhappy with the way the world is and tend to be critical of our own and other leaders and how they are handling these issues, which might be global warming, the Middle East, terrorism, Africa, the economy, and so forth. When we feel rejection or hate toward whatever is in our reality, we actually energize and increase it. We actually empower whatever we hate or whatever we allow to bother us in any way.

How might we be contributing to these national and global realities?

1. First of all, our leaders are simply a manifestation of our group consciousness. When our consciousness changes, our leaders will change. We need to look into ourselves to understand why we have the leaders we do and how we empower them.

2. Another way that we contribute is through our dependency on comfort and material things. All of these require oil, water, and heat and deplete the natural resources of the earth. Our

addiction to these comforts causes us to give much money, and thus power, to the conglomerates that produce them, and they in turn have the ability to control the governments. We are giving our power (through money) to the businesspersons who are controlling the politicians who are making the decisions. Our lifestyle is directly responsible for global warming and policies that have to do with a need for oil.

3. Our personal identification with the small group of persons we feel comfortable with and our alienation from people from other religions, races, or nationalities reflects in the situations in Kosovo, Ireland, the Middle East, Africa, and all over the world, where people from different groups are fighting with each other. They are a reflection of the fact that we do not yet feel the same unity with all religions, races, and nationalities—or even social classes.

4. The unjust and biased misuse of power in the world simply reflects our own misuse of power as parents, spouses, employers, etc. Few people have learned to use their power in a totally just and unbiased way. Our governments are simply doing the same. They are nothing more than reflections of our own state of evolution—or lack thereof.

5. We can never know what we would do if we were in another person's position. If a foreign power came into and occupied the USA or Europe, would we be pacifists or terrorists until they left? Were the early Americans, who ambushed and killed the British, terrorists or freedom fighters? On the other hand, if we were the leader of a country and someone bombed us and killed our people, could we do nothing about it? Most often the actions of both sides in these conflicts are extreme, unjust, and unenlightened, but they are the exact reflection of our personal tendencies. It is easy to judge others when we are not experiencing their situation. This judgment only increases what is happening.

6. All of our problems start with the illusion of our separateness from others, which then leads to fear, self-protective mechanisms, alienation, and indifference to how others are fairing. We become imprisoned in self-serving lives with a basic mistrust of those we do not know or of those who are not like us. This in

itself is an illusion that attracts a wide variety of personal and social realities. Political and religious leaders add to these fears and mistrust by reinforcing the idea that only we have the truth and that the others are bad and want to do us harm. When we are functioning in such paradigms, we are contributing to the social and world situation as it is.

These world situations are simply reflections of our own mental tendencies that need to be purified and evolved with Ho'oponopono and other methods.

We Are All in a Process of Growth

As souls in the process of becoming more emotionally, mentally, and spiritually mature and enlightened, we attract to ourselves situations that offer us the opportunity to learn the next lessons we need to learn in our evolutionary process. Of course, we have the free will to learn from these situations or not to. We have the option of holding on to our pain, fear, guilt, and anger, or we can let go of all that as we upgrade our perception of reality and move into forgiveness, self-acceptance, love, and peace.

Some of the situations we are attracting are for the purpose of learning these lessons. We may *not* have done something in the past to warrant what is happening. We may have chosen, as souls, for this to happen because we can use it to let go of fear and old dysfunctional beliefs and move forward. In such cases we are responsible, not because we have harmed someone, but because we have chosen this as a growth process. In such cases we can ask forgiveness or simply free the other or the life situation from the need to be that way any more because we have learned the lesson that we are responsible and that we can love whomever or whatever it is. Having learned to love, we do not need the lesson anymore.

We Are All One Spiritual Consciousness

Most religions teach that we are ultimately all one with the Divine and that in the Divine we are one. St. John the Evangelist quotes Christ as saying, "I am in you and you are in me and I am in the Father and Father is in me." Eastern religions are even more emphatic in declaring that we are actually all expressions of one divine consciousness. We are one consciousness, which seems to have split into many, as does the light of the projector at the cinema appear to break up into many different beings and their interactions on the screen. We are all projections of one divine consciousness, which is ultimately interacting with itself through our actions.

We, however, have the free will (or won't) and power to hinder the purity of that expression, and we are in a process of purifying and evolving our ability to express our true spiritual nature. We are all evolving together, and each person's success in that process benefits us all. On the other hand, each person's refusal affects us all.

Ho'oponopono is a process in which we recognize that we are not yet enlightened, that we still are attracting realities based on ignorance, memories, and programmings. Having realized this, we ask forgiveness from or thank the phenomena we are attracting and reestablish the state of love, which is based on the truth that we are actually one being. Then we thank the Divine for removing from us whatever may be other than love.

Conclusion

Ho'oponopono is a process in which we realize that

1. We are attracting all that is in our reality for some reason – it is not by chance.

2. We are co-creators of all that is happening personally and socially.

3. Everything is as it should be for the moment—as a stimulus to correct something in ourselves.

4. We can correct ourselves and, by doing so, affect the others and the whole.

5. We do not need to know what we are correcting in ourselves. We do *not* need to know what it is in us that is resonating with whatever has our attention.

6. The causes of our reality are either in the subconscious as memories, programs, or lessons we have chosen to learn.

7. The solution is the removal of inner causes for ourselves and others.

8. When we free ourselves from any aspects that are contributing to what is happening, then what is happening is less a function of us and more of others' lessons.

9. Freedom from memories and programs allows inspiration and enlightenment to come.

10. The solution is love for others and ourselves.

11. This is the goal of life—a road to enlightenment.

****

A possible phrasing for Ho'oponopono would be as follows:

Dear _____ (Person, situation, attribute, animal, society, group of persons, etc.)

I realize that I am a co-contributor to this common reality.

I ask forgiveness for anything in me that might be contributing to this situation.

or

I thank you for all of the opportunities for growth that you have given me until now.

I love you.

I love myself.

I release you from the need to be this way any more for my evolution.

I thank the Divine for removing from me anything that might be contributing to this reality.

Chapter Eight

Learning to Live in the Present

During any trying times, it is especially important to keep our mind in the present. We will be happier, more peaceful, and more capable of dealing with situations and solving any existing problems, as well as preventing any future ones. The point, or power, is in the present. We cannot act in the past or the future.

When we live in the past, we tend to be caught up in bitterness, pain, injustice, rejection, anger, or even shame and guilt. When we live in the future, it is usually with anxiety and fear.

In order to get free from our self-limiting minds, we will first need to weaken the stranglehold that time and space have on it. Quantum physics has told us since the early 1900s that time and space, as we perceive and use them, are actually illusions created by our false perceptions. They are limiting illusions that we have agreed to respect and abide by while incarnated on this plane. They simply do not exist as we perceive them.

The mind creates and is bound in these two dimensions, preventing us from experiencing the freedom and bliss of consciousness free from time and space. The solution is to learn to live in the present—free from the illusions of the nonexistent past and future. The only reality is the present one. Not even one second ago is real. Only this ever-present moment is real. The next second in time never comes. When it "comes," it is always this second in time. And now, this second. And this second.

Letting Go of Fear and Anxiety

Fear and anxiety are always about the future. If you analyze why you have anxiety or fear, you will realize that it is because you are focused on something that *might* or might not happen.

Anxiety has to do with fearing that we will not be on time or will not be able to complete something on time or that the result of our effort will not be as good we believe it must be in order for us to feel worthy and secure.

Fear is the result of our identification with the body and personality. We are afraid because we doubt our self-worth and safety. We fear pain and the death of the physical body. We fear rejection and feelings of unworthiness concerning the personality. What we fear is always something that has to do with what might happen in the future

We are not free to be happy when we experience anxiety about our own or our loved one's health, relationships, success, or well-being. We are projecting our fears and limitations into a possible future, actually making that possibility more probable as we energize what we fear. This does not mean that we will always create what we fear but that it is simply better to focus on what we would like and not what we fear might be.

At a lecture that I was giving on anxiety, I asked the audience, "How many of you have experienced anxiety over ten thousand times in your lives?" All of them raise their hands. Then I asked, "Of those ten thousand times, how many of you have found that what you feared actually happened more than ten times?" Very few raised their hands. I continued: "Now, of those ten or more times (out of ten thousand times you felt anxiety) that what you feared actually happened, how many of those outcomes that actually occurred were unsurpassable, impossible to overcome or solve, and are still problems in your lives today?" The answer was none.

We can see here the ineffectiveness of anxiety and fear. We experience it many times a day for so many years and yet only .1 percent of the time does what we fear happen, and even then our life goes on. Of course we might feel pain and other negative feelings, but the human soul is greater than any possible event or situation. This is evinced by so many people who have recreated their lives after losing their loved ones, work, homes, fortunes, and means of survival in catastrophes, war, or displacement. So many people have also continued with creative and meaningful lives after losing a limb or important organ.

Not everyone continues on with will power. We have free will. We can suffer and hold on to our feelings of pain, bitterness, injustice, and powerlessness. Or we can reach into the divine power in the center of our being and move on step by step.

Try this simple exercise:

Make a list of all of your anxieties and fears of whatever you fear may happen.

Now as you read that list, say to yourself, "Since the beginning of history, millions of people have gone through that and have found the power to recreate their lives. I will do everything I can to create the life I desire for myself, my family, and the society in which I live, while I remember that I have the power to live a happy, meaningful, abundant life in all situations, regardless of what happens."

Living in a Loving Universe

We need to come to the point where we feel confident that

1. The future will bring to us and our loved ones only what we have chosen as souls and what is best for our evolutionary process. These events and situations will be our opportunities for growth, creativity, and the fulfillment of our life purpose.

2. We are immortal, Divine Consciousness temporarily focused in these bodies, and we have the power to deal with whatever might happen. We cannot die; we can only withdraw our consciousness from these temporary bodies.

The most effective way to free ourselves from these self-limiting negative emotional energy fields that bind us to the past and future is energy psychology. We can dissolve them with various methods, such as EFT, TFT, TAT, BSFF, WHEE, Sedona method, Freeze Frame, and Ho'oponopono, as well as others.

Reconciling with and Accepting the Past

Obviously we need to let go of all pain, fear, bitterness, resentment, anger, shame, guilt, and self-rejection in relationship to the past. One way to do this is to dissolve the energy fields created in the past that are now residing in what Eckhart Tolle has named the "pain body." These fields cause us to recreate external and internal situations in which we relive these familiar emotional states. We become addicted to, and thus limited by, these past experiences and then tend to recreate them.

The pain, bitterness, shame, and guilt from the past are like heavy sacks on our backs that do not allow us to stand straight and move forward and create and enjoy the lives we deserve. We are limited by these negative energies, which are burdening our endocrine, nervous, and immune systems, and compromising our psychosomatic health.

By holding on to negative emotions toward others, we harm ourselves more than anyone else. In addition to harming ourselves and our health, we also emit negative energy which, according to the law of attraction and sympathetic vibration, attracts to us behaviors, events, and situations that tend to augment what we are already feeling.

Realizing That the Past Was Perfect

You might reject this idea, but it is your only freedom from this weight of the past. Everything that has happened until this second that you are holding this book and reading these words is exactly what you co-created with your thoughts, beliefs, emotions, words, behaviors, and actions along with your soul choices to learn certain lessons. Nothing has ever happened to you that was not allowed by the divine laws of justice, wisdom, and love or was not your soul choice. We are the sole (or soul) creators of our reality. No one has ever been responsible for our reality, and we have never been the creators of their reality.

Each of us is doing the best we can with our ignorance and the programming that limits our ability to be who we would really like to be. How many times have you decided to behave or live in a different way, only to find that your attachments, beliefs, habits, fears, and other programmed emotions simply do not allow you to behave as you would like?

The same is true for the others. They, like us, are doing the best they can, considering their past. Not one person in our past could have ever done any differently, considering their limitations and the soul contracts we made with them for our mutual evolution. The same is true concerning our actions. We also did the best we could with the beliefs and attachments and the soul contracts others had made with us for their evolutionary processes.

This does not release us from the responsibility to always check with our conscience every moment, asking ourselves, "Am I doing to others what I would like them to do me? Am I avoiding doing to others what I would not like them to do to me?" This is the law or frame of reference for all actions.

The Power of Forgiveness

We can now realize the immense power of forgiveness of others and ourselves. We need to forgive everyone, including ourselves, for whatever we have done until his moment. This does not mean that there are no unjust acts, only that there are no victims. For example, you could, out of fear or pain, behave to me in a way that you would not like me to behave toward you. That would be an unjust act. But it could not happen to me if that was not something that I chose or needed for my own evolutionary process. I am not the victim. I have created and chosen these conditions for my growth process. You are simply the means.

You are responsible for your unjust actions and will need to free yourself from whatever causes you to behave in this way, but you are not responsible for my reality. Thus it is easy to forgive you because you cannot do anything to me that it not my creation or choice.

You would benefit much more by forgiving yourself for your unenlightened actions and, rather than spending energy on rejecting yourself and fearing punishment, seeking to discover what caused you to act in this way. Then you can heal that part of yourself, using this opportunity for moving to another level of consciousness, where you do not need to behave this way in the future.

In this way, we forgive others and ourselves and become reconciled with, and free from, the past. When these emotional energy structures related to the past and future are dissolved, we will be free to enjoy the happiness, peace, and aliveness of the ever-present moment.

The Power of Acceptance

The key to happiness is acceptance. Pain and fear are the result of fear, nonacceptance, and resistance to the past, present, and future. When we do not accept what has happened to us, or what we have done or not done, we are in resistance to the past. This creates an inner tension that obstructs our happiness in the present. The same occurs when we are resisting what now exists in our lives. When we feel negatively about our life situation, including our work, finances, state of health, and, of course, relationships, we are in an antagonistic relationship with our life and are not free to enjoy the present.

We equally resist the future when we have specific attachments and fears that cause us to desire specific outcomes and dread and fear others. We fear that what we want and need as personalities may not manifest and that what we fear will happen instead.

How can we accept the past, present, and any possible future? Faith in some basic spiritual truths is the answer. Let us reiterate once more these truths that are so important to remember when we are not feeling well.

1. We are all immortal spiritual beings who are temporarily projecting our consciousnesses into these physical vehicles for the purpose of evolving our ability to express our divinity here on the physical level. Our permanent nature is not this form, but rather formless consciousness. Thus we actually have nothing to gain or lose here. We are never actually born and never die. We simply project (are born) and withdraw (die) our consciousnesses from this physical realm.

There is nothing that has happened or could happen in the future that in any way will change who or what we are and have any real effect on our true formless nature. Thus, there is absolutely no need to reject or resist anything that has ever happened, is happening, or will ever happen. The only reason we resist is because of fear.

2. Spiritual laws allow only those events and situations into our lives that correspond to what we have chosen spiritually or created on some level of our being as opportunities for growth, learning, and evolution. Nothing has ever happened or can ever happen in the present or future that is not exactly what we have chosen (at some deeper spiritual level) or created as a growth opportunity. Fearing or resisting what we ourselves have chosen or are manifesting does not make much sense. This same truth applies to our loved ones for whom we are concerned.

3. We and our loved ones all have the inner power to deal with whatever might appear in our lives. We, however, have the free will to use or not use that power.

4. Whatever we might ever encounter in life, even our worst fears, has already been encountered, dealt with, used as a growth opportunity, and transcended by many of our fellow beings on this earth.

We can be happy now!

In order to live in and enjoy the present, we need to be free from the idea that we will be happy when some particular prerequisite we have in mind is satisfied. Perhaps we believe that we will be happy when we have the love of a certain person or more money or success at a certain endeavor. We keep telling ourselves that someday when *that* happens, we will finally be happy. And when we have all that we seek at this moment, we will probably feel that we need something else.

We need to let go of such illusions and realize that we can be happy right now—with our lives as they are. Happiness is an inner state that we can experience any time we allow ourselves to, regardless of external circumstances. The truth is that others on the planet are allowing themselves to be happy with the same exact situations that we are rejecting and creating pain about.

We ourselves create these false prerequisites or attachments, and we program ourselves to believe that we cannot be happy until something precise happens, such as having the specific spouse or money we need. We give the power to those external factors to unlock our inner happiness. For example, we say to ourselves, "I cannot be happy without that specific spouse." And yet there are six billion other persons on the planet who are able to be happy without that specific person. How is that? And today, in a time where people change relationships, the specific person we think we must have in order to be happy changes from time to time. It is simply an idea that we program ourselves with—nothing more.

One of the most important phrases from the Course in Miracles is "I give to everything the meaning it has for me." Each of us has become programmed to give a different meaning and amount of importance to the various aspects of this physical world.

We need to learn to be happy with our present just as it is. That is true freedom. Once we have done that, then we can much more easily manifest what we would like now, without fear of what will happen if we do not get what we want. The law of attraction states that we manifest what we feel strongly about. When we strongly desire something but also strongly fear not getting it, we are sending out two mutually canceling messages.

Once we have found inner peace, self-worth, and happiness in the present, feeling gratitude for all that we have and all that has happened in our lives, we will be able to attract whatever we choose. Self-worth, security, fulfillment, and happiness are *in* us, and we can continue manifesting all that we need to be happy as long as we accept and feel reconciled with the past, present, and every possible future.

Freedom from What Others Think

Happiness also requires that we be free from anxiety about what others think about us and our lives. It means being free to be who we are in all situations.

We do not need to get free from others but rather from our own fears and attachments. Happiness is our destiny because it is our true spiritual nature. That is why Christ emphasized that we need to become like children—free and innocent as children, free from programming and what others think. Free to be natural at all times.

As we move forward on our spiritual path, we will once again become like children, authentic and in the present. This, of course, must be distinguished from being reactive or rebelling. When we rebel, we are bound to *not* do what others want us to do, or we are bound to do what they do *not* want us to do. That is not freedom. That is not spontaneity. That is being bound to being reactive and not inspirational. When we act from inspiration, we are free to do what we really want, regardless of whether others approve or not. We are not bound to doing what others want, nor are we bound to not doing what they want. We are free to be who we are and to do what really serves our happiness and growth.

Testing times require even greater awareness of the truth and of the present moment so that we can be positive, using all that is happening as opportunities for our own self-knowledge and freedom from false beliefs.

Remember the difference between the pessimist and the optimist:

The pessimist sees the problem in every opportunity.

The optimist sees the opportunity in every problem.

Which do you choose to be?

Focus on the Breath, the Senses and Your Energy Field

There are three points of focus that help to bring us into, and keep us in, the present. They are as follows:

1. The breath – whenever you find that your mind is wandering into the past or future, become aware of your breath, of the air flowing into and out of your nostrils. You do not need to control your breath, but simply be aware of the process of breathing. Practice this as you walk, as you are waiting in lines, as you

are cleaning the house or working in garden. Be careful not to overdo it when operating a car or other potentially dangerous machine.

2. Your senses can ground you in the present. Focus on what you are seeing, hearing, smelling, feeling, or tasting. Enjoy the sensations – allow them to stimulate you and keep you alive in the moment. One of the reasons we become addicted to the sense pleasures is that they bring the mind into the present and free it from the pain and anxiety of the past and future. So when you are thinking negatively or too much, focus on your present environment. Look around and actually see what you are looking at. Listen to what you are hearing. Enjoy what you are smelling. This will relax you and simultaneously make you more alive.

3. Experience your energy body – your inner body. In chapter three you learned how to do deep relaxation. In this state of relaxation you can become aware of your energy body. You can learn to feel this energy in this state and then remain aware of the energy—especially in your chest area—as you act and perform your daily responsibilities. When you have mastered this ability, you will be able to be aware of this energy field in your chest area while engaging in your daily activities. This will keep you in the present.

Pain, anxiety, and fear are mainly based on the past and the future. Remember these three keys to the present: your breath, your senses, and your energy. Keep in the present as much as possible and all will be well.

CHAPTER NINE

Letting Go of Negative Emotions with the Sedona Method

Hale Dwoskin makes the following description of his mentor, who created the Sedona Method:

"In 1952, Lester Levenson fell critically ill. His doctors informed him that he had only a few weeks to live. Lester turned to the laboratory within, seeking a way to revoke his pending death sentence. What he discovered in his exploration was that by releasing his non-love feelings, his health began to improve. Continuing with this experiment, he found that over a 3-month period, he had attained not only renewed health but actually perfect health and perfect peace of mind which lasted 42 years beyond his doctors' expectations. It was from this state of mind, as well as his working with people over a 22-year period, that he inspired the creation in 1974 of what is now known as The Sedona Method."

This method is very simple and yet very effective. It can be applied at any time, anywhere, and with various levels of depth. We will present you with a very brief explanation here, which obviously does not replace the official course, which can be found at http://www.sedona.com.

The simplest and quickest version is to focus on any unpleasant emotion, such as fear, guilt, pain, rejection, anger, or hate and ask yourself four simple questions:

1. Can I accept this emotion?

    The answer to this question is not always a yes, as we have learned to reject, suppress, and feel shame, guilt, weakness, self-rejection, and even anger at ourselves when we feel negative emotions. It is not actually necessary to answer the question. Asking yourself is sufficient. If you can, in fact, cultivate a feeling of acceptance toward the feeling and toward yourself with that feeling, that will help with the letting-go process. The rule is that it is difficult to let go of what we do not first accept.

2. Can I let go of this emotion?

Allow your answer to come forth naturally, remaining unconcerned with what it is. Believing that you can let go of it will help.

3. Do I want to let go of this emotion?

There may be parts of ourselves that do not want to let go of this emotion. We may have become used to it and have identified with it. Perhaps we believe that we need to be the victim in order to be worthy or to be angry in order to be right or protect ourselves from others. Or perhaps we have the belief that as long as we feel guilty, we are good people. We may fear letting go of this emotion.

Again, we do not need to answer yes in order for the method to work. Just allow the answer to come forth by itself.

4. If you would like to let go of it, then when would you like to?

This may seem to be a silly question, but ask it anyway. When would you like to let go of this emotion? Do not be concerned with the answer.

Now that you have asked these four questions, go back and check on the emotion to see how strong it is. If it is still there or has been replaced by another emotion, then ask the same four questions until you become clear and peaceful.

A Clarification about Letting Go

When we say "let go," that does *not* mean that we fight or try to push out the emotion. It means that we cease holding on to it—that we let it go just as we cease holding on to a rock or pen. There is no effort involved— only a surrendering up of what we feel, allowing it to expand like energy and perhaps dissipate on its own.

We are not our emotions. They are energies created by our beliefs and programming. Once formed in our energy field, the natural evolution would be for them to flow and dissolve, as do all other forms of energy in the universe. For example, heat does not stay where it is, but flows in all directions until it dissipates and is no longer centralized. All energy follows these laws of flow, distribution, and dissipation.

Young children who have not learned to hold on to their feelings can be very angry at, or hurt by, one of their friends and then, after ten minutes, be playing with him or her as if nothing happened. This is the natural flow of emotional energy.

It is obvious from these examples that our emotions are not holding on to us, but that we are holding on to them. Letting them go means that we realize that we are not them and that we can choose to accept them as they are and let them flow, decentralize, and dissolve.

Discovering the Sources of Our Emotions

Basically, all emotions are based on fear and guilt. We feel fear, pain, injustice, bitterness, hate, jealousy, and anger when we fear that our basic needs or attachments are in danger. Our most basic needs are security, self-worth, freedom, control, and pleasure. When our belief system interprets some behavior, event, or situation as threatening to these basic needs, we feel some of the above mentioned emotions. Other persons who have other needs or different ways of fulfilling them will not have the same emotions concerning the same situations.

The fewer our needs and attachments, the fewer our negative emotions. Attachments are the ways in which we feel that our needs must be fulfilled. We might become attached to the approval and love of a certain person and think we need it in order to feel worthy or secure. Another person might be attached to money and appearance and need it in order to fulfill his need for self-worth or security. Our attachments are created by beliefs that dictate, "I cannot feel secure, worthy, free, happy, fulfilled, relaxed, in control without _____." Each of us fills in this blank with different attachments. Thus our emotions are created by our attachments, which specify and limit how our needs must be fulfilled.

Doubts, Needs, and Attachments

Our needs and attachments are created by our doubt concerning our security, self-worth, freedom, and control. If we did not doubt these, we would not be attached to external prerequisites in order to feel them.

Our doubts are created by the fact that we have lost contact with our inner security, self-worth, freedom, and wholeness. Having lost the awareness of our true spiritual self, our doubts create attachments to certain means of satisfying our basic needs, which can never actually be satisfied externally.

The solution, then, for letting go of each emotion, is to discover the need, attachment, and doubt that is creating it, and learn to let go of that. Once we let go of our doubts concerning ourselves, and the attachments to certain external situations created by those doubts, we will be free from those emotions.

Letting go of doubt, attachments and needs

The process once again is simple. We focus on the emotion and ask ourselves the questions below:

(When we use the word "attachment" here, we can also mean need or doubt.)

1. Which attachment do I subconsciously believe is in danger here?

2. Is it my self-worth, security, freedom, control, or pleasure, etc.?

3. Can I accept that I have been programmed with this attachment?

4. Can I let go of this attachment?

5. Do I want to let go of this attachment?

6. If yes, when would I like to let go?

Now as you focus on the attachment or doubt, see if you can simply let go of the need to fulfill it in a specific way. Allow yourself to feel your own inner security, self-worth, freedom, happiness, pleasure, etc. without the attachment.

When we let go of a need, attachment, or doubt, we do *not* let go of its content, only the need itself. Needing something is exclusive to having it. Having something removes the need for it. We cannot have self-worth as long as we need it. We cannot feel security as long as we doubt it or feel the need for it. The same for freedom and control and all other needs. We let go of the need and doubt, but not the feeling itself.

By feeling our own inner self-worth and security, we are able to let go of the doubts we have about them and the need for specific external factors for us to feel them. We satisfy our needs from within and thus are free from the needs and the emotions they generate.

This process is enhanced by allowing a light to flow through us, removing all doubt and filling us with self-worth and security. Allow that light to fill all your body and mind, creating within you what you have been seeking outside yourself until now.

This method allows us to let go of our false beliefs and experience our true spiritual self. This is what enabled Lester Levenson to heal himself from sure death and live another forty-two years.

This method can be employed at first as a type of inner exercise in a relaxed and concentrated state. Eventually, however, once we are familiar with it, it can be done in just a minute as we mentally observe ourselves and ask those questions and return to our inner center. We can do this as an inner dialogue even while working and interacting with people and life.

Letting Go of Positive Emotions

You may find it strange that you are encouraged to also let go of positive emotions in the same way. The reason is that most positive emotions are products of the same conditioning and inner doubt that creates our negative emotions. We feel happy and worthy because our attachments and needs have been fulfilled externally and our doubt has temporarily subsided. Entertaining the positive emotions based on the satisfaction of our needs only sets us up to feeling pain when they are not externally satisfied.

Of course, this is you own decision. You may feel that you need to feel positive at this time and have no desire to let go of those happy feelings, even if they are based on external conditions that will surely change at some moment. This is your choice.

I can only verify that every time I have employed this method on positive emotions based on needs being externally satisfied, I did not lose any positive energy but was uplifted to a state beyond happy and sad—a state of peace and bliss beyond these opposites. It has always been something even more wonderful than what I let go of.

This simple method is an invaluable tool during emotional times. I hope that you will give it a chance. For more information, go to http://www.sedona.com.

CHAPTER TEN

The Importance of Gratitude

Let us focus once again on the importance of gratitude, discussed briefly in previous chapters. Few realize that gratitude is the key to happiness, abundance, and spiritual development—especially in testing times. Most of us experience more pain and resentment about what we do *not* have than gratitude for what we *do* have. When we worry and complain about what we do not have or what is not as we would like it to be, we automatically lose awareness, appreciation, and enjoyment of all that we have and take for granted. We are less free to enjoy what we have.

According to statistics circulating on the Internet (which I cannot prove or disprove, but seem likely to be true), if you are reading this you can count yourself among the blessed and lucky on this planet.

Here are some of those numbers that should make us realize how blessed we are:

80 percent of our brothers and sisters on this planet live in poor living conditions

70 percent are illiterate

50 percent are uneducated

1 percent have computers

1 percent have higher education

If you have a reasonably healthy body, you are in a better position than the one million persons who are ill and will leave their bodies in the next seven days.

If you are not living through a war, in prison, or in hunger, then you are much luckier than the 500,000,000 who are living in such conditions.

If you have food, clothing, a home, and a bed, then you are in a better position than 75 percent of the souls incarnated on this planet.

If you have a bank account and money in your pocket, then you are among the lucky top 8 percent of humanity.

So much of what we have taken for granted simply is not so for most of the humans on this planet. There are so many souls living without much of what we cannot imagine being without.

Gratitude is the acknowledgment of the love that we are receiving from the universe in the form of loved ones, belongings, comforts, and abundance of all forms. Acknowledging the abundance we already have is the first step to attracting more. If we are ungrateful for what we have or are unhappy, complaining, or bitter, then we are sending out into the universe a negative message, which attracts more negativity; more of what we do not want and less of what we want.

No one enjoys an ungrateful person. No one—not even the Divine or the universe—is inspired to give more to an ungrateful person.

Gratitude increases with spiritual development. As we grow in consciousness, we naturally feel grateful for the small things, such as a breeze on a warm day, clean water to drink, good friends. As we evolve and learn to trust more deeply in the wisdom of the unfolding events in our lives as opportunities in our spiritual growth process, we even begin to feel grateful for initially difficult or unpleasant events or situations. We are grateful to persons who might test our love, forgiveness, self-acceptance, or understanding, for they are giving us invaluable opportunities to let go of our fears and ego and remember our true spiritual nature and, of course, *their* spiritual nature.

We can learn to feel grateful for physical and economic problems that test our inner sense of security and self-worth. We do not in any way seek such experiences, but, when they appear, we use them gratefully.

Gratitude is directly related to love and happiness; we experience love when we feel grateful and are grateful when we feel love. The same is true for happiness. We are happier freer beings when we acknowledge how lucky and blessed we are.

You would not be reading this if you did not already have enough security and abundance to get the book and enough time free from the challenge of survival to sit and read. Otherwise you would be searching for safety, food, shelter, and other basics needs. We need to discover ways to remember all that we have and get into the habit of feeling grateful many times daily.

One way is the gratitude rock mentioned in the book and movie *The Secret*. We could, however, use any object with which we come into contact many times throughout the day, such as a stone in our pocket, a bracelet, a chain around our neck. Alternatively, or additionally, we can place a sign on our desk, mirror, TV, or refrigerator; something that will cause us to remember all that we love and are grateful for.

We can set up a system of being reminded by a sound from our watch, mobile phone, or computer, or a specific place that we pass a number of times daily that would cause us to remember. Or we can connect gratitude with a specific activity such as brushing our teeth so that all the time we are brushing we are thinking of all that we can feel grateful for.

The more we do this, the more it becomes a very powerful habit. This is a feeling that transforms our lives. By feeling grateful for all that we have—even what is sometimes initially unpleasant—we are transformed into happy, beautiful beings. When we are happy and grateful, we attract people. We are pleasant to be with and we are easier to love because we love more easily.

We attract more positive realities from the universe. Gratitude is the one most important energy we can emit when seeking to attract what we desire.

We have already suggested that you make a gratitude list and have it next to your bed where you can add to it and read it every morning before getting out of bed or every evening before sleep (or both).

While making your list, consider the following lists created by two people (one male and one female) who did the exercise. As you read this list, remember that even kings and queens did not enjoy many of these sources of pleasure and security 150 years ago.

After reading the following list, totally ignore it and make your own as it flows from your heart.

- For my parents who supported and cared for me until I was able to survive on my own—and then let me free.

- For my siblings with whom I have shared and experienced so much.

- For my children—and all children—who give me such joy with their innocence and wonder.

- For my life partner with whom I share mutual support and share in life's challenges—and even more so life's joy and laughter.

- For previous friends and lovers with whom I have shared and learned.

- For my relatives, friends, and acquaintances with whom I have shared friendship.

- For coworkers, employers, and employees, with whom I have shared the common goals of our work environment.

(I am grateful to all of the above mentioned souls with whom I have chosen to have a special relationship in this life, not only for those positive moments, but also for those moments where their behavior has given me the opportunity to see my fears, attachments, and weaknesses, and to learn to put myself in the other's position and to understand, forgive, and love.)

- For my eyes and the ability to see and derive so much pleasure from this beautiful world.

- For my ears and the ability to hear so many pleasing sounds.

- For my nose and the ability to enjoy smells of all kinds.

- For my taste buds that allow me to enjoy delicious tastes.

- For my skin that allows me to get pleasure from so many sensations.

- For my brain and mind that allow me to receive and enjoy all of the above.

- For my pets and other animals, especially birds, which make my life more beautiful and enjoyable.

- For my home, which protects me from the sun, rain, snow, and other elements.

- For my bed, where I rest and rejuvenate in safety.

- For clothing that protects my body.

- For shoes that protect my feet.

- For food that sustains my body and mind and gives me enjoyment.

- For my refrigerator that protects my food.

- For my stove where I can prepare my food.

- For all kitchen and household appliances that make my life easier.

- For my computer, which gives me much enjoyment and is a tool for creativity.

- For my TV and DVD and CD players, which give me so much pleasure.

- For my car and other machines that facilitate my needs.

- For running water in my home.

- For electricity in my home that allows me all the comforts of all the appliances and machines that serve my needs.

- For all of nature—the trees, flowers, butterflies, rivers, beaches, forests, mountains, seas, and oceans, which give me so much peace and pleasure.

- For special places in nature that I especially love.

- For all animals and other beings on this planet that beautify our lives.

- For documentaries on animals and plants that leave me spellbound and in wonder at the wisdom and power of nature.

- For my education, which has helped me understand the world more clearly.

- For my books as sources of knowledge and enjoyment.

- For the Internet—as an invaluable tool of learning and communication.

- For all the teachers, gurus, and guides who have lead me to my true self.

- For music of all kinds that relaxes, inspires and uplifts me.

- For dance because it makes me feel alive and allows me to express parts of myself that I cannot express in any other way.

- For theater, television, and cinema because they open my heart and allow me to feel through others, and also fill me with feelings and enjoyment.

- For all the persons who have created the above mentioned forms of entertainment and information.

- For all colors, materials, clothing, jewelry, and objects of beauty.

- For special foods that I especially enjoy.

- For groups of people that I share time with because, through sharing, we experience trust, acceptance, and love.

- For all doctors and psychologists who are dedicated to helping me and others in their search for health and happiness.

- For all the waiters and waitresses that have served me and others.

- For all the cooks who have prepared, with love, food for me and others.

- For all the maids in hotels who have cleaned my rooms.

- For all the clerks in stores that have helped me find what I need.

- For the people I pass in the street.

- For my telephone, mobile, and other forms of communication.

- For the birds singing in the trees.

- For the wind, the earth, the water, and the sun.

- For all the techniques that have helped me get free from negative emotions so as to experience inner peace and happiness.

- For all of the spiritual teachings, truths, and wisdom that set me free from my illusions and fears.

- For sports that I enjoy playing and watching.

- For performances of all kinds that I enjoy.

- For affection, hugging, kissing, and sexual enjoyment with my life partner.

- For physical exercises, breathing techniques, prayer, and meditation, which keep my body and mind energized and in a state of well-being.

- For my body and its ability to move and take me where I want to go and perform the tasks that I find enjoyable and meaningful.

- For my mind that serves me all day long and enables me to understand and function in this world.

- For life after death and my immortality.

- For Christ and all other spiritual beings who have enriched and inspired my life with their teachings, but even more so through their examples.

- For women and men who, with their examples, have given me courage to face life's difficulties

- For those who have tested me with their behavior through the years and helped me to know myself, my weaknesses, and fears, thus giving me the opportunity to transcend my ego and understand, forgive, and love.

- For people's mistakes and weaknesses that have also enabled me to see my own.

- For difficult moments in the past and present that have strengthened me and increased my self-knowledge and inner strength and peace.

- For all the wonderful moments of love, happiness, laughter, and play that have deepened my trust and love for my fellow beings.

- For those peaceful moments of sharing with loved ones.

- For the support, acceptance, and forgiveness I have received from others throughout the years.

- For all of those who share the same interests with me.

- For those who have been born into other religions, races, and nationalities, and allow me to discover our innate oneness behind all those superficial differences.

- For the blooming flowers and the abundance of fruits and vegetables.

- For the sea, which rejuvenates and frees me.
- For the wind that caresses and cools me and opens my nostrils.

Now make your own list and add to it daily.

CHAPTER ELEVEN

Methods for Increasing and Balancing Our Energy

During testing times, our energy is often depleted physically, emotionally, and mentally. It is essential during such times that we take even greater care of our energy level. Following are some brief suggestions as to how we can create a healthy and harmonious energy level.

Which methods and life styles from the list below are you interested in investigating and employing? You may already be familiar with these methods. You may have already made decisions in the past to employ them, yet may not have been as regular in attending to your health and well-being as you would have liked. In that case, you might want to ask yourself: What has prevented me until now from loving myself enough to care for my energy level as much as I would like?

(For more details on each of the suggestions below, refer to www.HolisticHarmony.com.)

1. Proper diet. Few of us realize the powerful effect of a proper diet, not only on our physical health, but also on our emotional, mental, and spiritual states. A pure diet can create greater health, more positive emotional states, clearer mental functioning, and increased spiritual alignment.

2. Vitamins. If we suspect our emotional state may also be the result of a worn down nervous system, we might benefit from a strong multivitamin and mineral supplement for one month.

3. Fasting. We can dramatically improve how we feel with short one-day fasts, or a "mono-diet," during which we eat only one type of food, such as only apples, watermelon, grapes, or perhaps brown rice. When fasting, some may experience an increase of symptoms if a healing crisis is provoked. A beginner in this process should be assisted by an experienced guide.

4. Herbs or flower essences. Some herbs can be very calming or invigorating, offering the calm or extra boost that may give us the optimism we need to make internal changes.

5. Daily physical exercise. The body is a vehicle, and like all vehicles it needs to move or it will begin to malfunction. Exercise is essential both for a healthy muscular, skeletal, and circulatory system, and also for a relaxed nervous system and balanced endocrine system. This systemic harmony is necessary for emotional and mental peace.

6. Breathing techniques are essential and very effective for an abundant flow of vital energy throughout the body and mind. Bio-energy is the basis of all physical and mental functions. Breathing exercises are one of the most effective ways to increase our energy level and keep it steady and harmonious so we will be less susceptible to low emotional states or illness. We should, however, start with an experienced guide.

7. Daily deep relaxation will calm the muscles, nerves, and all other bodily systems, and thus rejuvenate the body and the mind. Deep relaxation, in combination with the above-mentioned techniques, contributes to the development of a strong and healthy immune system as well as being a form of self-therapy from psychosomatic illnesses.

8. Creative self-expression is much more important to our physical, emotional, and spiritual health and harmony than most people imagine. We are creative beings. Our purpose on Earth is to create. We might create a family, a business, a farm, a painting, a piece of music, a dance, etc. Creative self-expression is essential for our health, harmony, and happiness.

9. Meaningful activity is also necessary for us to feel that our life is worth living. When we do not perceive what we are doing as meaningful, useful, or helpful in some way, we are more susceptible to depression.

10. Massage. Shiatsu massage, polarity massage, spiritual healing, Reiki, and other such energy-oriented types of massage can be especially effective in relaxing the nervous system, reducing negativity, and freeing up the flow of bioenergy.

11. Cleansing techniques. One simple method is to increase the number of showers or baths you take. Contact with water can be healing and calming. We can also benefit by cleaning the internal bodily systems with enemas and other internal cleansing techniques.

12. Emotional release. We might need to partake in a program of emotional release under the guidance of an experienced professional who can help us release pent up emotions—especially pain and anger—that undermine our health and energy level.

13. Social harmony. We need to discover and overcome any fears or beliefs that prevent us from feeling comfortable with others.

14. Spiritual orientation. Each of us has his or her own personal relationship with the universe. Whether or not we adhere to any particular religion, it is important for our inner balance that we feel and cultivate our relationship with the whole as we perceive it, such as humanity, nature, consciousness, energy, or God.

15. Self-knowledge. We need to understand our own inner mechanisms, needs, desires, fears, expectations, beliefs, and subconscious workings in order to free ourselves from the negative emotions and mechanisms, which undermine our health, happiness, and relationships.

16. Enlightening the subconscious. This aspect of self-improvement usually requires an experienced professional who can help us reprogram the subconscious with positive, more objective beliefs and perceptions of ourselves, others, and the world.

17. Energy psychology. These are extremely effective methods for freeing ourselves from negative emotional and energy fields that control how we feel, creating unwanted and self-limiting negative emotions. (EFT, TAT, TFT, BSFF, WHEE, etc.)

18. Unconditional love. Love itself is the ultimate source of positive energy toward ourselves, others, and life in general.

You may now want to make a program for caring for your energy, health, and well-being. Try to be as specific as possible. On which days and at what time will you be employing which methods? Be realistic and make a program that is feasible for you at this time. Also, avoid the trap of "I will start tomorrow" because tomorrow never comes. There is only today.

CHAPTER TWELVE

Using the Freeze-Frame Method for More Inspired Solutions and Alternative Perceptions

Scientists at the Institute of HeartMath in Boulder Creek, California, did numerous studies in order to understand the physiological effects of the Freeze-Frame technique that they developed for their patients.

These results were published in the following scientific journals:

The American Journal of Cardiology

The American College of Cardiology

Stress Medicine

The Journal for the Advancement of Medicine

Here we will present you with a brief explanation of how to employ the technique. For details and scientific studies, go to their Web site at http://www.heartmath.org/. The data quoted here is from that site and their publications.

Briefly, they found the following results on those employing the technique:

1. Their heart rhythms improved.

2. Their nervous system became more balanced.

   (Sympathetic-parasympathetic balance)

3. Beneficial changes occurred in their hormonal patterns.

4. They had a marked improvement in their immune system response.

5. They evinced a significant shift in how they thought and felt and dealt with problems.

Why Were They Motivated to Do This Research?

The need to discover a technique such as Freeze-Frame was based on the following scientific and medical facts:

1. 75 percent to 90 percent of all doctor visits in the United States today are for stress-related disorders.

2. Job stress has become "the 20th century disease" and is considered a global epidemic.

3. Depression was the fourth leading cause of disease burden in 1990, and by 2020 it is expected to be the single leading cause.

4. Acute stress ("fight or flight" or major life events) and chronic stress (the cumulative load of minor, day-to-day stress) can both have long-term health consequences.

5. As much as 80 percent of all disease and illness (in the United States) is initiated or aggravated by stress.

6. According to a Mayo Clinic study of individuals with heart disease, psychological stress was the strongest predictor of future cardiac events, such as cardiac death, cardiac arrest, and heart attacks.

7. A Harvard Medical School study of 1,623 heart attack survivors found that when subjects got angry during emotional conflicts, their risk of subsequent heart attacks was more than double that of those that remained calm.

8. Three 10-year studies concluded that emotional stress was more predictive of death from cancer and cardiovascular disease than smoking; people who were unable to effectively manage their stress had a 40 percent higher death rate than nonstressed individuals.

9. In 1996 a study on 240 middle age men in Finland who filled out hopelessness questionnaires showed that those who felt hopeless were 2 to 3 times more susceptible to early death.

In Which Situations Can Freeze-Frame Help Us?

1. Whenever we are overcome with negative emotions such as fear, hurt, guilt, confusion, or anger.

2. When we are trying to solve a problem.

3. When we are in a relationship conflict.

4. When we are trying to create something but are feeling blocked.

5. When we have lost our peace and clarity.

I suggest that you use this method whenever you are looking for an alternative solution to any type of a problem, whether it is emotional, practical, economic, or even spiritual.

How Is the Technique Performed?

The technique described below is a somewhat modified version of the classic method described in the HeartMath booklets. Using it has led us to this variation. For the classic method, go to their Web site.

1. Stop. Take a time out so that you can temporarily disengage from your thoughts and feelings—especially the stressful ones. (This is why it is called Freeze–Frame—from movie terminology meaning to stop the frame and look at it and perhaps make an adjustment in it.) Focus on the issue that you would like to deal with more clearly or more effectively. You are freezing the frame concerning this issue so that you can step out of it and examine it more clearly, thus enabling you to find an alternative way of perceiving it and dealing with it.

If you are experiencing negative emotions concerning this issue, then you can employ aspects of the Sedona method here by remembering that you are not these emotions. Accept them and then allow them to expand, flow, and dissipate. This can be done for two to five minutes.

2. Now focus on the area of the heart energy center in the center of your chest. Imagine as you inhale that your breath is coming in through the center of your chest and when you exhale that it is flowing out through your solar plexus (just below the sternum). As you do this, imagine energy or light coming into your chest on the inhalation, feeling that you are filling your chest area with light and peaceful energy. Imagine that you are exhaling out of the solar plexus area. You can do this for three to five minutes.

3. Now bring to mind someone you love. This could be a member of your family, a friend, or perhaps an aspect of the divine that you love, such as Christ. Or it could be a beloved pet or even a part of nature such as the sea, a favorite flower, or music. As you focus on this object of your love, allow your heart center to be filled with the feeling and energy of love. Let go of your other feelings and resistance and allow yourself to feel love, appreciation, and gratitude. This can be done for three to five minutes. You have now created positive feelings and thought frequencies, which cause the mind to relax, become clearer, and function in an improved way.

4. Now bring the original issue that was causing you concern at the start of this exercise into your heart center and allow alternative perceptions, feelings, and methods of dealing with this to enter into your mind. Here you are not so much thinking as letting go and allowing new alternative perceptions and feelings to come forth from the place of peace and love in your heart center. You might also ask yourself, "what would be an efficient, effective attitude or action that would relax me and perhaps solve this issue?"

5. Remain in this state of inner peace as long as you enjoy it.

6. Now imagine yourself employing this alternative means of perceiving, feeling, and acting.

What Results Did They Find in the Laboratory?

In the lab it was found that experiencing these positive feelings provides the following:

1. Rejuvenation of the immune system

2. Health and well-being

3. Increased clarity

4. Greater discernment

We have found this to be an invaluable technique for changing our emotional state and perception. It is used by the staff in many companies as a means for greater effectiveness and problem solving. I hope you will give it a try.

CHAPTER THIRTEEN

Being a Light Worker Is the Key to Real Happiness, Success, and Abundance

Everyone is trying to be happy. It's the main goal of every human life. In order to be happy, we need, among other things, security, safety, contentment, acceptance, affirmation, respect, freedom, and love. All day long and even during our dreams, we work hard trying to create these very illusive and rare states of mind. What portion of humanity has succeeded in this challenge? Do you know many people who feel enough security, contentment, acceptance, and love in order to feel really happy most of the time?

Let us look as some facts collected by Anup Shah on the site Global Issues about the reality we, as humanity, have created until now: http://www.globalissues.org/article/26/poverty-facts-and-stats.

We give value to what we believe is important. Our beliefs and values dictate where we dedicate our time, money, and energy, thus creating our personal, social, and collective reality. The factors that indicate our real values are how we spend our time and our money. These priorities are responsible for the present state of humanity. We have, with our present value system, created this economic crisis and a very substandard reality for ourselves and our fellow souls on this planet. Consider the following facts concerning our values as indicated by our spending.

Consider the global priorities in spending in 1998:

Global Priority	$U.S. Billions
Cosmetics in the United States	8
Ice cream in Europe	11
Perfumes in Europe and the United States	12
Pet foods in Europe and the United States	17

Business entertainment in Japan	35
Cigarettes in Europe	50
Alcoholic drinks in Europe	105
Narcotics drugs in the world	400
Military spending in the world	780

Now compare the above expenditures with what is estimated that we would need to manifest basic education, clean, sanitation, nutrition, and health services in all developing countries:

Global Priority	$U.S. Billions
Basic education for all	6
Water and sanitation for all	9
Reproductive health for all women	12
Basic health and nutrition	13

In other words, in order to have basic education, water, sanitation, health, and nutrition for all the developing countries we need only $40 billion or 2.8 percent of the $1418 billion that we spend on cosmetics, ice cream, perfumes, business entertainment, cigarettes, alcohol, narcotics, and military spending.

These are our values in action. Imagine that your family had these values and you spent 97 percent of your family's money on cosmetics, ice cream, perfumes, entertainment, cigarettes, alcohol, narcotics, and security and did not have any left for educating your children, for water and sanitation or for the healthcare of your family members.

This is what we members of the family of humanity have chosen. This is one of the main reasons why we are going through this economic crisis. Our test at this moment is to reconsider our values and life styles. Our test is to realize that we are all unique aspects of one Divine Consciousness, just as all the cells in our bodies are unique expressions of our bodily consciousness.

Consider the following information:

1. **Water problems affect half of humanity**

   - 1.1 billion people in developing countries have inadequate access to water.

   - 2.6 billion lack basic sanitation.

   - Almost two in three of the people who lack access to clean water survive on less than $2 a day, with one in three living on less than $1 a day.

   - More than 660 million people who live without sanitation live on less than $2 a day, and more than 385 million on less than $1 a day.

   - 75 percent of the poorest 20 percent of humanity do not have piped water into the household.

   - 1.8 billion people who have access to a water source within 1 kilometer, but not in their house or yard, consume around 20 liters per day.

   - In the United Kingdom the average person uses about 150 liters a day.

   - The average water use in the United States is 600 liters a day.

   - A mere 12 percent of the world's population uses 85 percent of its water.

2. **Being a child in our world**

   - Some 1.8 million children die each year as a result of diarrhea.

   - Close to half of all people in developing countries suffer from health problems caused by water and sanitation deficits.

   - Fifty percent of the 2.2 billion children in the world live in poverty.

   - 640 million children are without adequate shelter.

   - 400 million children have no access to safe water.

   - 270 million children have no access to health services.

- 121 million children on this planet are not receiving education.

- 10.6 million children died in 2003 before they reached the age of 5.

- 1.4 million die each year from lack of access to safe drinking water and adequate sanitation.

- 2.2 million children die each year because they are not immunized.

- 15 million children have been orphaned due to HIV/AIDS.

3. Our cities

- In 2005, one out of three urban dwellers (approximately 1 billion people) was living in slum conditions.

- Indoor air pollution resulting from the use of solid fuels, by poorer segments of society, claims the lives of 1.5 million people each year, more than half of them below the age of 5: that is 4000 deaths a day.

- In 2005, the wealthiest 20 percent of the world accounted for 76.6 percent of total private consumption. The poorest 20 percent, just 1.5 percent.

- 1.6 billion people—a quarter of humanity—live without electricity.

4. The distribution of wealth

- The GDP (Gross Domestic Product) of the 41 Heavily Indebted Poor Countries (567 million people) is less than the wealth of the world's 7 richest people combined.

- The world's billionaires—just 497 people (approximately 0.000008 percent of the world's population)—were worth $3.5 trillion (over 7 percent of world GDP).

- In 2004 about 0.13 percent of the world's population controlled 25 percent of the world's financial assets.

- Approximately 790 million people in the developing world are still chronically undernourished, almost two-thirds of whom reside in Asia and the Pacific.

What are we doing wrong?

What's wrong then? Why are we unable to succeed in this effort? How is it that as divine beings we have failed so miserably to create the beauty, abundance, happiness, peace, love, and unity we have incarnated to manifest? The answer is, once again, ignorance, fear, separateness, alienation, and selfishness. We are under the illusion that we are these separate bodies and that we are in danger from others and that we need to protect ourselves.

Cells in the Body of Humanity

We are all cells in the body of humanity. As cells, our purpose is to be healthy and vital so that we can serve the needs of the whole body, which means the other cells. Each of us as cells has a unique function in the body of humanity. When we are indifferent to the needs of the other cells in the same body, then we are like cancerous cells setting up that body for disharmony, illness, and death.

If we as cells hoard blood, nutrients, or oxygen so that they are not available to the other cells in the body, then we and they both suffer. As cells in the body of humanity, we cannot be well unless the other cells are also well. We are ultimately dependent on the other cells, and our state of being is directly and indirectly interlinked with theirs. The body's health depends on all cells selflessly serving the body. The body in turn sustains and gives life to all the cells. A cell cannot live well in an ill body. And the body will be ill if the cells do not perform their functions and instead serve only their own needs. We will never create the happiness and abundance we seek until all have equal opportunities for the same.

Become a Light Worker

How, then, can we contribute to creating abundance for ourselves and all the other cells in our common body of humanity? We need to become Light Workers, who share love, wisdom, and all types of material, emotional, mental, and spiritual support to those in need. We need to alter the misconceptions that have caused us to create this imbalanced reality. Let's examine some of them:

1. The belief that there are not enough resources for all of us to be content is one major obstacle to human happiness. Because we believe that there's not enough for everyone, we seek to take

care of ourselves and our close circle—often at the expense of others. This leads to competition, aggression, hoarding, selfishness, greed, accumulating food and money, and possessiveness while others have nothing. Then we wonder why others hate us and even attack us.

The truth is that there are plenty of resources on the earth for everyone to be happy, but they are not distributed properly. They accumulate in some areas and are lacking in others. The result is similar to what would happen to a human body if the blood accumulated in one part of the body and consequently was not able to reach other parts of that body. Both the oversupplied and undersupplied parts of the body would be damaged and in serious danger.

That's what has happened on the Earth today. Some areas of society are suffering ethically and also physically from having too much while others are suffering physically and mentally from having too little. In the end, neither is happy.

   2. We feel like an empty vessel that needs to be filled. Because we feel empty, lacking in inner happiness, security, contentment, and peace, we're motivated by the needs to take, to accumulate, and to fill ourselves with whatever we presently believe may ease the feeling of emptiness. What we believe will fulfill us gradually changes as we mature from dolls, games, and toys to motorcycles, the opposite sex, marriage, children, success in a profession, money, possessions, and social status.

On the humorous side, here is a chart that was traveling through the Internet:

What is considered success at which ages?

At 2 years of age:	At 80 years of age:
Not defecating on your self.	Not defecating on your self.
At 12 years of age: Having friends.	At 75 years of age: Having friends.
At 18 years of age:	At 70 years of age:
Having a drivers license	Having a drivers license
At 20 years of age: Having sex.	At 60 years of age: Having sex.
At 35 years of age: Having money	At 50 years of age: Having money

Now, humor aside, the common recipes for happiness have failed us. We've done it all. We should be happy now. But we're not. We could have much more health, communication, peace, contentment, understanding, love, and abundance. Perhaps we've been trying to find happiness in the wrong way?

Empty Vessels or Channels Connecting the Divine with the Material

Perhaps our basic assumption about the nature of life was wrong? Maybe we're not empty vessels but actually empty conduits, through which life is flowing. In that case, we cannot expect to create a static state in which we fill ourselves and remain full. We hoped that we could put something in our empty vessel, i.e., a new job, enough money, a pleasurable experience, acceptance, or love from the others, and it would remain there and we would always be happy after that. But it doesn't work that way.

Life is growth, change, and evolution. Static water begins to stagnate; fungus grows; illness takes over. The empty vessel approach is a denial of the flow of life; it is living death. Holding on to the past is not trusting in life. Not allowing life to flow through us is a result of not having faith in life, in Divine Justice, in Christ's promise that our needs will be met if we live in harmony with the will of God.

If we can imagine that we are, instead, an empty pipe, through which life and divine energy are flowing, then we will understand that security, contentment, and affirmation are dynamic processes in which what allows us to feel good and satisfied continually changes. We can then let go of the need to hold on, to accumulate, to try to control situations and people. Just because last year we felt secure or happy with some particular experience or situation doesn't mean that we must fight tooth and nail to hold on to this past source.

Human evolution requires an evolution in the objects that give us the feeling of security and happiness, too. The object or situation that we allow to be the key to our happiness and contentment continuously evolves until it becomes our relationship with the Divine or with our own inner self. Then, our sense of security, contentment, and happiness can never be in danger, for they don't depend on any temporary or changing stimulus.

Keeping the Flow Going

Let's assume that, in fact, we are really empty pipes that are connected at one end to the Cosmic Source of life and at the other to the physical reality we experience around us. Let's examine what we can do to keep this cosmic energy flowing efficiently so that we can always receive abundantly from the Source of all Good and Goodness.

The answer is simple: keep emptying the material end of the pipe. The more we give, the emptier the pipe is and the more we are able to receive. We create an internal vacuum by giving a portion of what we have to those around us. This vacuum then draws down more grace from the Cosmic Source, and we experience a continual state of abundance without anxiety, fear, worry, competition, antagonism, and the feeling of separateness, which pervades society today.

This may seem at first to be an illogical train of thought—that we actually can gain much more by giving than taking. We're not talking about taking only spiritually; we're also including money, security, food, safety, acceptance, knowledge, self-esteem, contentment, love, and happiness. This is not a new thought. Every religion has informed us of this truth, but few people have yet to believe it.

For the last two hundred years, we've been experimenting with the belief that affluence brings happiness. We see clearly now that this is not true. Ask your children if they believe that we've succeeded with our formulas for happiness. We've succeeded in becoming parasites on the earth, consuming inconceivable proportions of the earth's natural resources of oil, food, and minerals, only to leave tremendous amounts of pollution and waste that are destroying forests, seas, and whole species of animals, endangering harmony and life on the Earth.

And, in spite of all this, we are not happy. The family unit is disintegrating; marriages in general fail; love is scarce; and mistrust, fear, discontent, and anger are rampant in every level of society. Ask your children what they see and why they tend to reject this society and its ways—why they don't study, why they don't show respect to their elders and to society. What is there to respect? Where is there an example, a politician, a doctor, a lawyer, a teacher, a priest, a man, or woman about whom the child can say, "I want to be like him or her?"

Perhaps I'm getting carried away, but the time has come for drastic changes in our way of thinking and acting. Otherwise, our future as humans is doubtful. Let's now consider what we have to gain by adopting this different concept for obtaining happiness through giving.

Gaining by Giving

Giving to others includes many types and levels of giving. This might include money, clothing, food, books, furniture, or other objects, or time, compassion, ideas, love, friendship, work energy, prayers, positive thoughts, joy, a smile or any other type of physical, emotional, mental, or spiritual offering. The recipient of our giving may be the orphaned, the poor, the rich, the elderly, the handicapped, the blind, the deaf, the dumb, the seriously ill, the lonely, the distressed, or any other person or group that may need help from others.

How do we gain by giving in this way?

1. We diminish our concentration on the ego. By dedicating a few hours each week to others, we begin to put the ego in its proper place. We become freer from our ego needs, and our energy flows outward toward others rather than only toward our personal satisfaction.

Let us clarify that we are not advocating any type of conflict with, rejection of, or hatred for our body, mind, or ego. They are our beloved instruments for creating, communicating, manifesting, and interacting with others and the material world. We need to love and care for them and gradually perfect and educate them as to their actual purpose.

2. Giving allows us to let go of some of the attachments that rule our lives and force us to waste so many hours chasing after them. We also lose hours worrying about whether we'll achieve them or be able to hold onto them, or perhaps feeling bitter toward others who we consider to be obstacles to our fulfilling our attachments.

We need to understand the difference between the means to happiness and happiness itself. We confuse them. A new dress is not happiness. Neither is food, sex, a movie on TV, a new job, or a relationship. We *allow* these experiences to stimulate the feeling of happiness in us. We could allow other objects or situations to create those same feelings.

3. We develop a feeling of oneness and love with others. We all want love. When we are loved, we are especially happy. We

demand love from others and complain when they don't love us, but the surest way of getting love is giving it! Yes, it is 100 percent sure that those who give more love receive more love; that is, if we're really giving love without strings attached. If there are strings attached, such as wanting love back, wanting favors, needing the other for security or pleasure, wanting gratitude or for the other to fulfill certain expectations, then we may not get love back.

Giving allows us to feel close to others, to be concerned about their needs, their feelings, and their happiness. Our feeling of separateness gradually diminishes along with our feeling of loneliness. We feel unity with others, which is a sign of advanced spiritual growth. Those who feel lonely could easily solve their problem by serving those in need.

4. We begin to feel useful and our life has a new meaning. When we serve others, we are filled with a new inspiration for life. We realize that we have something to offer, that our existence has a purpose, that we can contribute in our small way to a better reality for others in need. If more and more people offered just a few hours a week to those in need, the whole world would be transformed. This would happen not only through the service offered but through the love that would be expressed and the new feeling of trust, which would develop among people. All would be more relaxed, less fearful, more at peace with themselves and others.

5. We begin to discover where we are holding on and where we are still attached. Serving others helps us to realize just how selfless or selfish our service is. When most of us start out this type of activity, we do it for ourselves much more than for others. Many criticize selfless service just for this reason, but the only way to learn to swim is to jump in the water. In the same way, we'll learn where we are attached or where our giving is conditional or egotistical by passing through the various tests of selfless service.

When we are in reality giving in order to make others love us, they may treat us very badly so that we can discover that we're giving with expectations. They won't do this consciously. Life will use them to teach us this lesson. When we're using this activity to boost our image in front of others, to gain approval and respect from others, it may backfire in our face; our goal may not be achieved. If we believe that the other should have gratitude for what we've done, he or she may show us exactly the opposite so that we let go of this motive. When we're attached to getting specific results from our efforts, life will teach us very quickly to let go of this attachment and to perform this action simply because we believe that it must be done. We do what we feel inspired to do and enjoy doing it. That's our reward, the joy of doing.

6. We engage the cosmic flow of goodness on earth. The more we give and let go, the more everything comes to us. Life begins to bring us the money, clothing, food, pleasure, wisdom, accep- tance, friendship, and love that we need to be really happy. All this comes to us *not* through our seeking but through our giv- ing. We become instruments of a higher power, which is work- ing through us in order to fulfill its purpose here on earth. We begin to feel a relationship with that higher power in our quiet moments of meditation, prayer, and eventually even in our mo- ments of activity. We feel it to be ever present, always supplying our needs, giving us what we need to be secure and happy while fulfilling our purpose.

7. We become Light Workers, or transformers of spiritual energy. A transformer changes one type of energy into another. Plants take the energy of sunlight and transform it into food energy. We transform spiritual energy into ideas, thoughts, words, and actions that bring abundance, contentment, health, happiness, and harmony to all.

When we dedicate more and more hours and energy to selfless service, we become enveloped in a blissful flow of energy in which we're contin- ually receiving from a spiritual source within us and giving out to those around us. We need less from others. We receive our support and sense of security from higher levels. We become Light Workers, sharing love and peace in a society that's suffering and afraid of the darkness settling in all around.

As Light Workers, we offer up all the results of our efforts to the Divine. We are instruments, not doers, not planners. The screwdriver and ham- mer are not concerned about how the building is going along. They just allow themselves to be used for the projects that must be executed. Nei- ther do we need to worry about whether our effort will bring results. The results are dependent on many other factors beside our effort. We can only ask ourselves whether what we are doing feels right and important to do. If so, we do it and forget about the results.

8. We come into contact with the real source of happiness. Real happiness comes with the dissolution of ignorance. No person who is still identified with the body, mind, and ego can experience lasting happiness. Our feeling of separateness is the major source of unhappiness and tension in the world today. All religions and spiritual philosophies affirm that the truth is exactly the opposite, that we are all projections of the one universal being called God. There is, in fact, only one Spirit, which is projecting itself as all these beings and objects that we see around us, in the same way that the sun reflects as the thousands of different images on thousands of bodies of water. All these images seem different and separate, but there's only one sun.

A feeling of inner happiness pervades our life as we feel a spiritual oneness with all beings, independent of their political, religious, or social beliefs or affiliations; regardless of their appearance, age, or sex; and independent of their attitudes or habits.

We begin to feel for the first time in our life unconditional love, which is the basis of real happiness. We need nothing else. Our needs have become very simple. We spend little time seeking to satisfy our personal needs, for our needs are always satisfied by life itself. We are in the flow, always enjoying life. We are a part of life, not cut off from it in our limited circle of identification.

Sharing with and serving those in need is a basic solution to our personal, social, and planetary problems. Governments and religions will not solve these problems. Only we as cells in humanity can.

So What Can We Do?

1. Seek out groups or nonprofit organizations that are serving those in need.

2. Dedicate a few hours a week to those persons or groups you feel more inclined to serve or help in some way.

3. Remember that each of us has something unique to offer. We all have the ability to listen and show interest in others. Some have money to share. Others have special skills, such as medical,

legal, carpentry, or plumbing skills. Others have the ability to tutor children. Some are equipped with psychological techniques for helping those in stress or those who have been traumatized. Others can cook or perhaps shop for those who cannot move freely. One could read to those who are sight impaired or too old or too ill to be able to read for themselves. There are so many ways in which we can heal our body of humanity by serving the other cells in that body and thus make the body a healthier environment for us all to live in.

4. Pray for those you are helping. Imagine that they may come into contact with the divine light energy within each of them that gives them strength and inner guidance.

5. Perform Ho'oponopono for all who you believe are suffering or causing suffering for themselves or others.

In this way you become a Light Worker and part of the solution rather than a part of the problem.

CHAPTER FOURTEEN

Creating Peace through Truth

It is totally natural to feel pain, injustice, bitterness, fear, hurt, anger, rage, and hate when we experience or observe the pain, suffering, inequality, and injustice that are rampant on our planet. It is natural to sympathize with one side and search to blame or feel anger and hate toward the other. It is also natural for some of us to tune out and become indifferent. An illness of our times is that we can watch actual, innocent people suffer or die daily on the media and be emotionally unaffected.

On the other hand feeling pain, worry, anger, rage, and hate brings about more of what we are feeling negative about through the law of attraction. When we are against something and feel strong negative feelings toward it, we actually energize it. Also, when we feel sorry for or worry about others, we activate more of the same realities for them and others.

What Is the Truth Method?

So what is the solution? I suggest what I have named the "truth method" for creating peace, harmony, and abundance for all. We simply need to remember, visualize, express, share, and employ these truths in our minds and lives.

What are those truths?

1. All beings, including ourselves and those we consider the abused and the abusers are all expressions or extensions of *one* Divine Consciousness, which most call God. One formless light creates *all* of the images on the movie or TV screen. All of the images, peaceful and violent, are equally expressions, creations, or extensions of the *same* light. Thus those who are conflicting with each other are actually, on the highest level, one being, one consciousness, and we are also one with them.

2. All of our fears, negative emotions, greed, problems, alienation, conflicts, and indifference toward each other are the result of our ignorance and feelings of alienation from each other and from our one common source of existence and basic inner

reality. This inner reality transcends all religions, nationalities, races, genders, political perceptions, and philosophies.

3. The solution is to remember our oneness, experience it, express it, and visualize others remembering their own true nature and, through that connection with their higher selves, behaving in a spirit of unity for the highest good for all.

4. Nothing "outside" ourselves is separate from us. All is a reflection of our common nature, collective unconscious, or shared morphogenetic field. We are all, in some way, participants in and responsible for whatever we see before us. There are parts of us, perhaps very deep, that contribute in subtle ways to those conflicts or events that we reject and tend to blame others for.

5. Everything happens to us and to others because we are creating, choosing, or attracting whatever it is at some deeper level as an opportunity for our evolutionary process. This does not mean that we need to allow whatever is happening to us or others if we perceive it as unpleasant, unethical, or unjust. We have every right and responsibility to find creative, assertive, dynamic (but always peaceful) ways to influence what is happening so that we contribute to its evolution into something more just and ethical—at least in our perception. However, we must first perceive the event or situation as exactly what we and others have attracted as a stimulus for growth and evolution toward the truth.

6. In some cases our or others' lessons will be to accept and learn to be at peace with what is happening. In others, our lesson will be to wisely and dynamically act (not react) to *change* what is happening. In both cases our lesson is to accept, forgive, and love ourselves and others regardless of ignorance and mistakes. Reinhold Niebuhr expressed this perfectly in his prayer, "Lord give me the strength to change what I can, the peace to accept what I cannot and the wisdom to know the difference."

7. The most effective way to correct the world around us so that it coincides with our highest spiritual and moral values is to believe that we can all evolve to that state of perfection and to visualize it. This can be done in various ways:

   a. Pray for all to be reconnected to their true spiritual selves.

    b. Visualize all connected to their inner Light—connected with their inner source of strength, wisdom, and spiritual guidance.

    c. Ask and thank the Divine for cleansing all human qualities (in us and others) that might be contributing to what is not in alignment with the highest good for all.

How Do We Employ the Truth Method?

1. We start by remembering all of the above. This allows us to let go of negative emotions, such as fear, worry, anxiety, bitterness, anger, rage, and hate, and thus we cease to participate in the maintenance of the old negative energies and realities.

2. Daily focus on all of those who are externally participating (we are all involved internally) in the negative events or situations, and imagine them with light in them. Imagine this light giving them strength, wisdom, and spiritual guidance, allowing them to overcome fear, pain, suffering, anger, and hate and to function as their higher selves in harmony with the highest good for all. Here it is extremely important to include the "abused," the "abusers," and all of the leaders of all groups.

3. Daily ask to be cleansed of any tendencies that might be contributing to what is happening, even in small ways and even if it is on the other side of the planet. We do this even if it seems impossible that we could have any conscious or subconscious participation in the event. This is the philosophy of the Hawaiian Ho'oponopono method and, because I realize that this point might sound strange, consider reading a more detailed explanation at http://www.HolisticHarmony.com/archives/capsules/hopono.asp.

4. Communicate this new, more universal and philosophical perception of events—and of how to participate more positively and effectively—to others through spoken and written word in every way that you can.

5. Forgive those who have harmed you. Forgive yourself and learn to love yourself and others as you are. For help in forgiving, you might want to read the chapter on that subject at http://www.holisticharmony.com/creatingpeace/forgiveness.asp.

6. Participate with others in expressing how you believe the world can be and how you would like it to be. Do not be against anything. Be *for* what you believe and know we can create it.

7. Help those in need in any way you can. Unity is the solution, and helping others in need is a physical expression of that unity. You can help with money, food, material objects, actions, words, or simply by being there and listening.

8. Meditate or pray daily (or both), and come into contact with the peace, wisdom, and guidance within.

9. Be an example of what you believe and profess.

Chapter Fifteen

Twenty-Five Ways for You and Your Loved Ones to Maintain Health, Happiness, Peace, and Abundance during Testing Times

Here is a summary of what we have presented in this book.

You will find additions and updates at http://www.holisticharmony.com/creatingpeace/.

The suggestions are separated into chapters so that you can easily find the details.

Chapter 1 – Remaining Healthy, Happy, and Positive during Testing Times

1. Remember that all situations and events are opportunities for becoming stronger and happier.

2. Whatever happens, you will always be among the lucky 20 percent of the souls living on this planet.

Chapter 2 – Caring for the Body

3. Eat fresh foods as much as possible, avoiding canned and preserved foods and white sugar and its products.

4. When your life situation is stressful or more energy-consuming than usual, try taking some multivitamins and other supplements to protect your body and mind from depletion.

5. Do the half shoulder stand daily in order to ensure that ample oxygen and nutrients reach your brain and nervous system.

6. Give your face and head a self-massage a few times a week to rejuvenate your energy and your appearance.

Chapter 3 – Strengthening the Mind

5. Do deep relaxation daily for greater clarity and contact with your mental powers.

Chapter 4 – Cultivating Positive Thoughts and Feelings

6. Remember

    a. You are immortal Divine Consciousness.

    b. Your mind creates your reality.

    c. Nothing is by chance.

    d. We have created and chosen all that occurs.

    e. We are personally loved by the Divine and by all spiritual beings.

    f. Everything that happens is an opportunity for evolution.

    g. You have the power to deal with all possible situations.

    h. Gratitude is the basis of positive creation.

Chapter 5 – Using Energy Psychology to Get Free from Fear, Anxiety, and Other Negative Emotions

7. Use E.F.T. and other forms of energy psychology daily to dissolve any energy disturbances, such as anxiety, fear, bitterness, or any other forms emotional or physical pain or annoyance.

Chapter 6 – The Twelve-Step Manifestation Process

8. Use the twelve-step manifestation process for attracting and creating what you need for yourself, your family, and those in need around you.

9. Be happy and grateful for what you have while you manifest what you further need.

10. Cultivate happiness in various ways. Learn to be happy in all situations.

Chapter 7 – Ho'oponopono and How to Transform Our Reality by Purifying Ourselves

11. Perform Ho'oponopono on any persons, behaviors, situations, or events that are not as harmonious as you believe they could be. This includes performing it for

a. Persons whose behavior bothers you

b. Persons and or situations that need healing

c. Aspects of your body or mind that need healing

d. Your own situations, such as health, finances, etc.

12. Remember that all that you see, and especially whatever seems disharmonious to you, is a reflection of something within you.

Chapter 8 – Learning to Live in the Present

13. Let go of the past and the future.

14. Bring your mind again and again to the present moment, to your breath, your energy, and your senses in the present.

15. Let go of the importance you give to what others think.

16. Forgive others for their ignorance and mistakes in the past.

17. Forgive yourself for the same.

18. Learn and use the power of acceptance of, and reconciliation with, the past, present, and every possible future.

Chapter 9 – Letting Go of Negative Emotions with the Sedona Method

19. Use the Sedona Method daily to accept and let go of emotions and the needs, attachments, and doubts that create them.

Chapter 10 – The Importance of Gratitude

20. Make a list of all that you could feel grateful for and read it daily, adding something new whenever you can.

Chapter 11 – Methods for Increasing and Balancing Our Energy

21. Select and employ the methods that suit you from the list of eighteen suggestions for keeping your energy high.

Chapter 12 – Using the Freeze-Frame Method for More Inspired Solutions and Alternative Perceptions

22. Employ the Freeze-Frame method when you need an alternative way of perceiving, feeling, and interacting with what you are concerned about.

Chapter 13 – The Key to Real Happiness, Success, and Abundance

23. Allocate a few hours a week to serve and help those in need.

Chapter 14 – Creating Peace through Truth

24. Select and employ those methods that suit you from the nine-step truth method for creating peace.

25. Above all, be happy. This is your challenge.

About the Author

American-born, Robert Elias Najemy is currently living in Athens, Greece, where he serves as director of the Center for Harmonious Living, which he founded in 1976. The Center for Harmonious Living serves 5500 members with classes and workshops designed to aid them in improving their bodies, minds, relationships, and life in general.

Robert has twenty-seven books published in Greece, which have sold over 130,000 copies. Nine of his books have been published in English and can be found on Amazon.com.

He is also the author of over 600 articles published in England, Australia, India, and Greece and has prepared 500 lectures and relaxation CDs and DVDs on the subject of human harmony.

He has developed a program of seminars for self-analysis, self-discovery, self-knowledge, self-improvement, self-transformation, and self-realization. He has trained over 300 life coaches in person and continues to train live coaches over the Internet.

This system combines a wide variety of well-tested ancient and modern techniques and concepts.

Najemy's teachings come from what he calls "universal philosophy," which is the basis of all religions and yet is not limited by religions.

His seminars include a variety of experiences including the following:

1. Basic psychological and philosophical teachings.

2. Self-analysis through specially designed questionnaires.

3. Methods of contacting and releasing the contents of the subconscious in a safe and gentle way.

4. Exercises, breathing, movement, singing, chanting, and dance for expression and release.

5. Methods for discovering and releasing through regressions (in relaxation) the events of the past, which have programmed our minds negatively and thus are obstructing our happiness and effectiveness in the present.

6. Techniques for solving inner and interpersonal conflicts.

7. Methods for calming the mind and creating positive mental states.

8. Experiences for feeling greater unity with others and breaking through feelings of separateness.

9. Opportunities to share with others what one is feeling and experiencing.

10. Emotional release techniques.

11. Methods of meditation and transcendence of the mind for those who are ready.

His material can be found at http://www.HolisticHarmony.com.

Other books and e-books by Robert Elias Najemy in English (available at Amazon and bookstores)

Universal Philosophy

The Art of Meditation

Contemporary Parables

The Mystical Circle of Life

The Miracles of Love and Wisdom

Free to Be Happy with Energy Psychology by Tapping on Acupuncture Points

Saram – The Adventures of a Soul and Insight into the Male Psyche

The Psychology of Happiness

CPSIA information can be obtained at www.ICGtesting.com
Printed in the USA
LVOW061802011111

253045LV00004B/238/P